RISE LIKE

∧

PHOENIX

How to incinerate beliefs that hold you back and rise from the ashes to live your best life.

Geraldine Mair

www.choosetoclimb.com

For my son Christopher.

The light of my life and a gift beyond measure.

Mum x.

'As the phoenix rises out from beneath the ashes, so too will you. Clad only in new resolute force with more resilience than ever before.'

Geraldine Mair

Contents

Rise like a phoenix:

I hope to open your mind, reinforce your understanding, and set you free from the shackles of conditioning, replacing it instead with unlimited possibility.

If, after reading this book, I contribute or awaken a part of you, then I am deeply thankful.
I hope the curiosity it will ignite within to learn new things, gives you the gift of unlocking what may have been hidden up until now.

.

I feel grateful and truly blessed to realise my dreams of developing this brand and the books that followed.
From this moment, I encourage you to start that journey by defining a vision for your new life.
You hold those keys in your hands now with this book, so let go of what holds you back and *Climb Forever*…

Love and blessings, Geraldine

Quote

'Become the best example you can during this lifetime, be one with a constant, never-ending self-improvement engine at its core. Accept responsibility and accountability for your actions, and you hold the power to alter and achieve anything in your life, so, let's RISE...'

Geraldine Mair

Introduction by Geraldine Mair

This book is the first step in your transformation towards a better life and is supported by two other volumes to give you a complete set from which to reference.

1. *RISE Like A Phoenix!*

2. *100 Ways to RISE and Live Your Best Life Volume 1*

3. *100 Ways to RISE and live Your Best Life Volume 2*
'You will never be more than you believe yourself to be', and you can only adjust this state of mind through the repetitive action of any task. Applying this process ensures new thought connections form in your brain that will ultimately shape new habits.

I offer you the opportunity of discovery within these pages, to cement those new practices deep in your subconscious mind, unveiling your *'authentic power'* as individuals. One that builds a bridge to your full potential during your time in this place.

RISE Like A Phoenix will open a world of wonder, one to support and nurture your deservedness and draw happiness, prosperity, abundance, calmness, control, discipline, encouragement, and success into your life.

'You will have the opportunity to examine your thoughts, question beliefs imprinted over decades by others and change negative perspectives into openings for growth. Everything is about perspective, and it is your thoughts, beliefs and values that drive that train. You can step onto the path others have discovered ahead of you and begin to emulate their lead—the avatars who successfully manoeuvred their way through the cracks that blocked so many others.'

Let me explain how to navigate the storms, rationalise your fears, step into your greatness and excel in all phases of your life. After everything I have learned during my own passage, I have discovered that even when I apply direction, focus, and passion towards my vision, I am often pleasantly surprised by what shows up. Start by reconnecting to your gut and listening when you get a nudge to push forward or hold back. This offers you the option to handle rough terrain better and find an outlet that works for you.

'I had no idea the power of carving out quiet time each day through meditation, walking, listening to uplifting material or inspirational music until I started to include it in my daily schedule.'

The clearness I have found from this has helped me discover what is essential in my life, and I choose now to give my attention and energy to what I enjoy instead of external drama.

'I choose to be empowered by a positive image of my ever-evolving future, by visualising that forthcoming state every day in my meditations, and I leave my past where it belongs, behind me.'

Getting stuck in emotions that drive a miserable vehicle on a continuous loop is no way to be. Settling for an unhappy life, whether that has manifested as a job you hate, a relationship that's become stagnant or toxic, a deep sense of unworthiness, or something else, *'you are making a conscious choice to stay in that camp.'* I promise you years from now; you will be bitter and resentful if it even takes that long to realise what *'you chose to tolerate'.* I am telling you this from experience and my discoveries, and I say it with love, change today and give yourself the chance to modify your direction and feel joy again.

'If you don't, you will affect everything you touch from this point on in a negative way, simply due to the disharmony you will feel daily within yourself.'

Your life will reflect that of a victim; you will blame others for your woes, you will be disappointed most of the time or envious of others who took a different path and are rising faster and higher into a life you dream of having. It's never too late, so stop using that as an excuse. I want to make you realise how precious and valuable you are; you deserve a life that excites and stimulates, one you look forward to pursuing daily. You must identify that inner shift when you feel it and work towards its attainment by taking small steps each day, so when the door of opportunity appears, you are ready to walk through.

'I invite you to read this book with an open mind; take note of my personal experience and get inspired enough, to make the mental adjustments in yourself that currently hold you back. Through the release of those emotional anchors, you can build a different truth.'

The reason you are reading this book is a sign you are curious and searching for the solution. Let me commend you for being brave enough to identify your failings and adopt the measures necessary to alter your course completely.

This is your chance to become a powerful creator in what you undertake from this point on. If you are in a situation that is causing distress or unhappiness, you are choosing to stay there through fear.

'You are unwilling to act and move away from what is hurting you; it is essential to remember what you choose to accept you are refusing to change.'

On some unconscious level, you are telling yourself that acting is much more painful than remaining where you are. Sadly, this is often the very reason people live a life of misery, sometimes for decades and end up with nothing but regrets. ***Don't let this be you!***

'It will take nerve; you will have to push down your fears and keep going anyway. Expect to feel uncomfortable for a while, as it is an essential part of the process to get you past the problem.'

Dig deep and silence your self-sabotaging thoughts, the ones that have prevented your elevation up until now. Become mindful of who you keep company with, as many people fear change, and if they witness someone around them diverting to an alternative path, they can be very insensitive and vocal about it. It's more important than ever to stay on track when this occurs, as your historical conditioning will raise resistance in you and can halt or interrupt your growth if you listen. When you decide to follow an alternative path, what becomes intolerable can never be determined by another person, even someone close to you.

'Always listen to your gut first, as your heart and head can continuously trick you into thinking you are making a mistake.'

The longer you have put up with a problem, the harder it becomes to move away from it, and yet vital that you should. Your awareness must become the fuel that drives you forward and not the weight that pulls you back. Stop holding on to standards on living a life you didn't even set; it's your choice to either take control or give it away. Achieving this level of consciousness opens doors and will show *YOU* what the world is ready to reveal. No one can do this for you; you will have to come to this decision independent of anyone else. I promise you though, when you change your mind, you change your life, and it's a miraculous transformation, one that brings into form so many synchronicities it will amaze you.

I ask you now to release your restraints and RISE Like A Phoenix…

Our Story

Our books and the company brand Choose to Climb came from a story my husband shared with me over a decade ago. After training to be a business coach, Derek became inspired to write a blog influenced by a business and financial mentor; the subject matter was to follow your passion despite the risks.

In Switzerland, there is a mountain range called the Pennine Alps, and the sixth-largest is the Breithorn. (German for broadhorn; its elevation stands at 4,164 m). Many have succeeded in reaching the summit; however, several have lost their lives in pursuit of this goal. The blog focuses on climbing this mountain, using it as a metaphor to scale your challenges in life.

At the foot of the mountain is the village of Zermatt. In its tiny graveyard, the souls who couldn't complete the climb are laid to rest there.

'This is not a place of sorrow or defeat but one of quiet confidence and power.'

One headstone of a young male climber only 17 years of age captures this energy best and reads.

"I Chose to Climb".

When I heard this, I said to my husband it would be an excellent name for a brand as you can choose to climb in all areas of life. When I started writing my books, I remembered the story, and I knew then the message I was trying to convey ought to be the starting point for our journey, and The Personal Development Company of Choose to Climb was born.

I give thanks for the dedication of those who chased their dreams and especially for the young man whose sacrifice became his legacy and the name we have adopted as our own. I hope those who read this story will let go of restrictions, fears, or beliefs that hold them back and choose to develop the courage to ascend their mountains, instead of ambling at the foothills where no progress can ever be made. So, regardless of the outcome or what lies ahead in the pursuit of individual excellence, make this the beginning of your new story and *"Choose to Climb."*

- CHAPTER ONE -

BEGIN

YOUR ELEVATION

As you move through this book, I will explain why you react the way you do and show you how to correct your behaviour when it veers off course. You will come to accept *you* create *your* own reality through *personal choices, decisions, and actions.* I suggest you read at least one of the accompanying volumes to this book, as it will quickly help to identify where your perceptions and beliefs live towards certain situations, as well as the behaviours of others and how you choose to react or respond to them.

This book combines and explains the science of the mind to give you a reliable, easy to understand foundation from which to build. I encourage you to read and listen to empowering information every day and continue your education using additional material readily available on this subject.

'Please don't think one person knows it all because they don't, including me.'

However, books like these can plant a seed of curiosity, one that pushes you to find out more. I have listed my suggestions at the back of this book for recommended reads by alternative authors, those who have enriched my journey and supported my conscious awakening towards better.

'Living in gratitude should be the very first thing you implement from this information.'

It can be one of the most insightful things you will ever really learn and enable you to see the world with vastly different eyes. Life today is unrecognisable to what I remember as a child, with so much variety and choice. Yet, with the speed of life, it also becomes evident how much goes unnoticed.

'Instantaneous gratification is felt in the moment but never lasts, and with it no real appreciation for the enjoyment of what has already entered your life.'

The ego is responsible for making you feel you need more to be enough, and it is down to an incorrect view and a perception, that others are superior because they have more. No one can make you feel this way except yourself; your thoughts are the fuel and ammunition to energise those beliefs; when you measure your worth against what you see in others, it erodes who you already are or have the potential to become.

'Continually looking for the next best thing is called striving and is not the road to contentment, fulfilment, or peace.'

You will never find your gratitude in someone else or the unnecessary collection of anything to impress. It lives within, and your awareness of it can bring you more joy than you ever knew was possible. The smallest act of saying thank you at the end of the day, even if it was a tough one, should become your new norm. This will equip you with the tools to see tomorrow is a new day and therefore, you can always find something to be grateful for.

When you live your life this way and enjoy each moment, there is no need to feel any adulation beyond that. Awareness and appreciation of what surrounds you, will stop you looking outside at what others have or who they represent as a measure of your worth; you will already know you matter and have a contribution to make.

'This lets you find pleasure in the simplest of things, many you no longer take the time to notice, from the glistening carpet of dew on an early morning to the youthful memory of snowflakes falling all around you on a winters day. The excitement of sledging and building snowmen with your siblings and friends, or a summer's day lying on the beach without a care in the world and contentment for nothing but the sand between your toes. Re-connect with all of this through the lens of childlike wonder and your life will shift exponentially.'

Becoming an adult shouldn't make you unaware, choosing to feel overwhelmed by responsibilities, work, worries, and running around on empty, continually drains and causes nothing but stress. Taking just a little time to reflect and plan your days, can help you gain perspective on priorities, and this can help you release the weight and the ridiculous standards too many operate on to feel significant.

I spent many years believing the same things, and it's exhausting, only with the benefit of time, experience, and hindsight, it's easier to see how it contributed to unnecessary pressure!

'Any success you pursue in life must be measured personally, and not one built on someone else's vision. You

pick the goal, you act, and you bask in the rewards of that regardless of how large or small the wins are.'

There are many people today who were raised and still believe success is endowed or gifted, an illusory scale all worth's are measured by. Only for a select few, with the proper credentials, qualifications, financials, or connections. Yes, it's true, on the surface, some people seem to glide smoothly through life compared to the rest, yet what you see isn't always an accurate picture. There are often hidden stories just under that exterior, of individual tests regardless of their reputation, status, or affluence. When you evaluate the lives of others against your own advancement, you become the judge and jury of personal perceived failures, often not rooted in anything tangible. The truth is none of this is factual; you learned these beliefs growing up. Those restrictive thoughts that made you feel less and kept you trapped in fear were because no one taught you an essential life lesson.

'You are gifted, yes, every single one. You must be ready to self-educate to release your potential and let go of restrictive thoughts and beliefs that limit you. The only way to identify how magnificent you are is to learn how to create a new

construct in your mind, one with the potential to take you from where you are now, right up into the stratosphere.'

You *can* release conditioning that originated from your environment, social circumstances, influencers, and media channels. You connect what you see and hear as familiar to you, which creates the experience you live in each present moment. When you do not reach a level you had hoped for, you must find logic in your natural environment to make rational sense of it *so you can remain blameless*. It is an inherent human protection mechanism to stop you from having to take ownership of your choices.

'These are benchmarks from your past deeply embedded in your subconscious mind, and where you place the responsibility to comprehend your surroundings. It also becomes the reason you feel you can never be more than your reflection shows. It's an internal lie you formed over an extensive period of time.'

Unfortunately, it can leave a frustrated soul, full of disappointment when what manifests is the opposite of what you wanted. Continuation through the repetition of this process generates casualties of compliance. This places you into a holding pattern where there are no alternative options.

The familiar will continually rise to greet you again and again formed by earlier genetic patterns passed onto you; this causes a rhythmic model to emerge and begin to stack.

'You become enmeshed through old beliefs from hereditary ways that prevent any movement towards better. This is not because you don't want to, it's because you don't know how.'

Those boundaries now contain your field of perception that you currently operate within. You must take ownership and accountability for yourself, for until you do, you will be unable to develop the awareness of who, and what you could become. Setting the wheels in motion towards your best future will begin when you start taking motivated action to generate the impetus for you to want more. This attitude and approach have weaved within it, the potential to alter the trajectory of your very life. It's time to pay attention to any uneasy internal emotional signs, ones that are always there regardless of your upbringing.

'You know when you feel bad, or when you are in the wrong career or relationship, this isn't something I need to tell you; it's the job of your intuition. Understand you are in denial, which stops you taking any action required to change it. Begin to release the restrictive thoughts by asking yourself

what you believe and how that belief got inside your head. I guarantee it came from someone else and not you!'

Conformity *(to behave in accordance with socially accepted conventions)* how so many choose to live. When you come of age and do not actively educate yourself in the ways of the mind, you fall prey to an environment that wishes to keep you in chains. Independence of thought is accessible when you see your beliefs and values are just like a computer file; one somebody else wrote the programme for.

'Accepting you are the sum of past conditioning, thoughts, feelings, and behaviours, let's you appreciate your expectations are either mobilising or immobilising. Therefore, practising self-awareness can help rationalise, clear and release those immobilising anchors.'

Finding your way back to self-love is your first step to this awareness. If you can manage this step, you will be well on your way to finding you're authentic power and releasing old habits that restrict you. The love you cultivate internally raises self-worth and is necessary to reveal your ideal self *(the person you are at your source minus the negative coding).*

There will always be various paths to find your purpose; whatever decision you make regarding this, be sure it brings you joy, fulfilment and satisfaction, for you will need it to sustain your future in your chosen field.

'I honestly believe the best life you can cultivate will be one that nurtures your passion, through service towards the growth of others via your contribution.'

Look out for any interior nudge that repeatedly calls to you, one you ponder over for hours or something you marvel at in others, not from envy but admiration; this is your signal calling you to act. Choosing to follow these principles will always show you the road to reveal your bliss. I urge you to promote to others the fundamental value of pursuing dreams, utilising those talents, and the necessity of sharing them with the world. For you can only become your ideal self when you allow this truth into your experience. A conscious person invests time in personal growth by understanding it is the only way to comprehend the world around him. It becomes the most significant lesson in how to cut old cords and habitual patterns.

New thoughts can now flourish from a more organic platform; What you can achieve will astound you when the fears fall away.

'Follow the path, and no matter what life brings, there should be nothing to cause you to violate those terms, or at the very least cause you to pause and consider your options.'

This is how you can all revise your view of propaganda. With a new perspective, you will understand how the messages from media networks streamed through devices daily, programme the subconscious mind every moment you spend there. These sites have become a platform for various individuals to promote separation, violence, and misinformation.

' Refuse to buy into this fear, or you risk opening the very impressionable door of your mind that can become easily tainted. When you know who you are and you have enough rational perspective on your environment, you will have no desire to tolerate or entertain this.'

Teach your children the world is a beautiful place, full of wonderful people, happy to get along with everyone else. Thankfully, it's not the skewed pictures you see; it's a much smaller minority than you are led to believe.

'Your world can only mirror back what you give your attention to, so now you have this knowledge; I encourage you to limit this type of rhetoric and watch something else instead.'

A recent survey from the American Psychological Association found that for many Americans, "news consumption has a downside." More than half reported feeling anxious and suffered from fatigue or sleep loss from too much exposure. In the UK, the results are similar. There are many reasons that affect people's mental health during their lifetime; this modality is only one of them. However, If you are already struggling daily, the news channels will do little to alleviate your fears. Instead, they will reinforce your insecurities and worries. *At what point do you draw the line between your mental health and staying informed?*

These channels have multiplied exponentially from a few decades ago; the ability to live stream events or get a consistent notification on your mobile devices at any moment exposes you to an overload of information, with repetitive messages that are neither helpful nor positive. The amount of misinformation circulated within that vehicle is continuously training your mind to believe it. It generates more money, has more traction, and wins constant interest and attention.

'A powerful engine fuelled on fear creating the very dissonance that so many desperately wish to get away from. Harmful material of any kind has the power to create a spiral that can rapidly descend downwards, affecting your whole persona. It cements habitual beliefs that may already be there by convincing you this is how life is; it isn't, only what you choose to believe makes it so.'

Hopefully, you can see what drives most of the media feeds you watch. Learn to disconnect from this toxicity, and please believe in love again. Love for yourself, love for others and the good that can show up in your life when you remove things that harm your wellbeing. I have changed by investing the time required into self-education. I no longer watch or listen to too many of these things, choosing positive affirming material instead. There is little to be earned in spending endless hours debating pointless topics that hold no benefit. Languishing for too long in anything that affects your demeanour exposes your mind to the force within it; it might help to limit how much you allow into your day. Everything in life is better when based on balance.

'Direct your intention and align it with your attention, as both must work together to reveal your best path, instead of being swayed by peer pressure.'

When your focus is in a **'constructive direction',** and you have a personal desire to always stay above that line, you give yourself emotional permission to disengage from the negativity, which will vastly improve your outlook.

'You make a choice, and you continue with inspired action to reach for better every single day. Then you commit to following that calling for your whole life.'

Adopting this approach will take you to many incredible peaks on your journey during this lifetime. I wish you many extraordinary ones that leave you with incredible memories.

'Cultivate this skill, and you have the potential to enjoy a life of no limits and the prize of discovering your purpose for being here'.

Rise strong, accept and soar…

Geraldine Mair

- CHAPTER TWO -

THE REAL TRUTH

QUOTE

"There are going to be times you will find it very tough to accept the truth, even when it is right in front of you. When the evidence is strikingly clear, and it proves beyond a reasonable doubt, your beliefs are wrong.

You built this from neuro-synaptic structures over a long period. Based on fears and truths you formed. You have created an inaccurate picture of your authenticity, and it will be rooted in your need to either hold onto it or a frantic requirement that you must defend.

The only thing stopping your elevation is YOU."

Geraldine Mair

I was raised to accept there were ceilings in place I should never attempt to go beyond. My parents and peers were born in the early 1930s and did not come from affluent backgrounds. They were raised in a time of limited resources and conditioned to conform to the societies they lived in. When I was born, those mental constraints got handed down, as there was no awareness of anything else at that time.

'My upbringing in Roman Catholicism promoted fear, mainly from the religious creed I was taught, and it trained me to avoid risk. I have no disrespect in my heart for my parents or those who delivered this rhetoric over the years. I understand now people can only do their best with what is available at the time.'

Their conditioning from prior generations became their unconscious roadmap, and without any new information, it created a limited programme. When I began my self-development journey, this inevitably would uncover many alternatives and lead to questions that demanded answers.

'The discomfort I began to feel would make it impossible to follow anything that revolved around secrecy, cover-ups, dogma or doctrine, with trepidation at its core and heavily biased towards being the only right path to salvation.'

I began to understand how those beliefs had moulded my thinking and how necessary it would be now, to reclaim a new perspective starting with self-love. It would take me some time to build enough confidence to share my story, for I had to construct a brand-new mindset, one I was happy and proud to show to the world.

'This helped me grow, heal and transform into the person I am today, with a better understanding of how limited thinking in many areas of life can prevent you from seeing the truth.'

Many things in this world defy reasoning. I still believe in the power of creation and the creator, though no longer from a religious viewpoint but an inner knowing. I have no biased view towards anyone in this world who follows a particular creed or structured religion. I was a part of this for over forty-five years, and it's a personal passage and never for me or anyone else to judge? I believe now I was placed here for something less provisional than the rules that moulded my earlier years and decided after diligent research, my course would become one built from a different structure.

'It took me over five years to thoroughly study my religion, which created many questions, much doubt and internal reflection. Once the guilt subsided and that took a long time, I concluded this was the way it was supposed to be for me.'

17

I'm sure anyone reading this who experienced a similar upbringing might be able to resonate with the pain of separating from a community, one that was an intrinsic part of life for many, many years? I do not feel I need to go to a building to worship. I carry my faith with me and strive to be the best version of myself every day. I believe who I am is reflected in my behaviour, and I express those values in how I treat myself and others. I view everything in life now as a lesson or a teacher, and it has revealed many things through the application of these philosophies.'

My additional studies into the mind and personal development uncovered many hidden truths and assisted me in the hunt for better. Having navigated and transcended deep-rooted beliefs that hampered my individual growth, I have found my real purpose. I used to be someone who tolerated shoddy manners that hurt my heart and character. Through my education, I developed the competence to analyse things from an entirely different vantage point than I did back then.

'If you have found yourself in the same camp I did many times, I hope you will be able to let go of anything restrictive, open your eyes and step away from anything that violates that.'

I didn't do particularly well at school; I'm certainly no academic genius; I guess my disinterest in subjects like maths and chemistry would inevitably mean I would not excel in those subjects. I did, however, find enormous pleasure in anything creative. I enjoyed writing and journaling in my younger years and drawing for many hours on the corner of the sofa. As an avid ABBA fan in the late '70s and early '80s, it was a regular sight to find me singing in my room with nothing but a brush handle for a microphone. This was one of the happiest periods I can remember from my youth, the joy I had for the simplest of things, time spent with family and great friends, my love for school and the connections I made there. A genuinely untroubled time where all I cared about was living in the moment.

'I wasn't aware of how significant this side of me would become, and my talents would show up years later and turn out to be the catalyst to alter my course.'

I vividly remember one teacher (Deidre McFadden Rossi) who taught me English in high school. She was a woman who always used positive reinforcement and encouragement towards her students, helping them cultivate their creative flair. I can see with hindsight the direction she was trying to steer me in now. And I wish I had taken her advice sooner and followed a career in writing.

Like most teenagers, I had different ideas of what I was going to do with my life, and it didn't involve penning stories. It took me over thirty years to answer that call and create the books now available to come into form.

'It's often the little things you remember, a kind word, an encouraging person, someone who sees the potential not yet visible to you.'

Sadly, she was taken too young, and I never got the chance to share this with her, for she was one of the best teachers I had during my school years, a great inspiration, and a lovely lady.

The expectation in our family was to find work as soon as possible after leaving school. As a kid from a working-class background, the idea of a university degree didn't even enter my thoughts. It was a lot harder to get in back then anyway, as you needed a lot of money and exceptional grades to obtain a place. I didn't know anyone who was going, so I did what I learned how to and followed the only roadmap I had. My artistic flair was always encouraged and praised. Yet, there was an undeniable undercurrent that careers were not built using these skills and the ability to make money this way would be almost impossible. This is where I grew the belief because of what surrounded me back then, that working for a boss and earning a salary was the only way to go.

'It never came down to following a passion or making your happiness a priority; instead, it was more centred around becoming independent and supporting yourself and less about how you managed to join those dots.'

My dad was a joiner and an extremely hard grafter. Mum was a housewife and homemaker and raised in an environment where the teachings weren't that different.

'The general rule was to find work and grind hard; this became the default and the way my environment trained me to make a living.'

I cannot lay the blame at anyone's feet for the direction my life took or the fundamental errors I made in several chapters of it. It wasn't until I learned to question my choices; I was able to break free of the box I had been trying so hard to fit into.

'In a small town where the majority thinks the same way, it unconsciously becomes your roadmap to the future.'

When those you spent most of your time with have the same values, beliefs and backgrounds, there is no awareness to think any different. It wasn't really until the birth of the internet I would discover a world of information through technology; Analysis of the facts allowed me to make more conscious choices, which would ultimately drive my future self in an entirely different way. If like me, you want a better life, you must never stop, never quit, never believe you cannot have a fantastic future, and although you might not see it right now, I urge you to embrace the journey no matter where it takes you, regardless of your past story.

You must be open and willing to see it, look for the signs continuously forming through those internal nudges, and learn the messages weaved within. Don't get caught up in a societal structure that continues to measure by only one vehicle. There are so many different qualities in each of you, and when harnessed correctly, encouragement can produce extraordinary results. So many people still assess academia as the benchmark for intelligence. This can't be right when the creative mind has so much to offer too.

Albert Einstein said, 'Logic will get you from A to B. Imagination will take you everywhere.' When you understand the workings of the mind, this will make more sense to you than anything else.

Using an antiquated system only creates separation and prevents personal talents from being celebrated because they don't fit into that frame. You need to become smart with regards to your skills and find the best way to express them. You can create a living doing what you love, for the passion you will feel for your life will consistently pull you towards better. Invest time to cultivate your gifts as it is life-changing, and whether you are aware of it or not, you will influence those around you by showing courage and commitment to follow your right path. I try every day to improve my personal bests. I still trip or fall short and catch myself slipping back into old habits.

'However, through the application of what I have learned, I can identify quickly when it happens and actively make amends to redirect my course. You too must go through the trials and perturbation that naturally comes when testing your boundaries of what feels familiar to you.'

I implore you to push on through and keep going even when it feels challenging to do so, for this is where transformation lies, and joy dwells. You have no idea how things can alter when you embrace these philosophies; I am living proof of this in my own life. I made a conscious choice to continuously learn new things and apply them to enhance that knowledge bank. Deciding to re-educate yourself with this material changes your perception of everything and opens doors you didn't even know were there. I am sharing all I know to help you recognise what is possible. I hope by the time you reach the end of this book, I will convince you to choose this path too.

'Stay humble and honest, and if you think you want to do what I have done, then get ready to feel uncomfortable for a bit whilst you navigate the rough terrain. You are at the beginning of your journey, and I do believe if you stay on course, nothing you need on the way there will be denied you.'

You can alter your awareness of the world through your participation in the creation of it. Everyone matters; everyone is important; I ask you never to look upon others with judgment, which only causes divisiveness. Try to avoid any activities or groups that actively encourage you to violate your values. This is not your truth but the coerced path of another. I invite you to put yourself first and stop trying to be a people pleaser to fit in; this is in direct opposition to who you are at your source and works against your ability to express your authentic self. You deserve your love and attention, so don't model yourself on a version of somebody else. It is a waste of the person you already are.

'Halt any interaction with anything designed to hurt you or requires you to fit in where you know you don't belong, for

there is no more significant personal pain than incessantly evaluating yourself against another's standards and coming up short.'

Differences are the very things that make you magnificent; this is the link that spans this world and joins everyone together through an invisible cohesive bond. Humanity is not made up of several different species. Open your eyes; you may be slightly different hues, but the same none the less. It is your experiences and internal programming that shape your values and beliefs of those distinctions. Your strength comes from respecting those variations and should nurture a fascination in you instead of any disharmony. You'll find the capacity to triumph when you surround yourself with those who believe there is enough for everybody, regardless of race, gender, creed, or colour and finds enormous pleasure in celebrating those wins with fervour. Understand energies are contagious, and passing on negative vibes helps no one. If you wish to emit only the good stuff, then look at your personal beliefs, especially if, on reflection, you know they came from a source outside of you. (*Most of the time, they do*).

You are responsible when others persuade you to do anything that disregards what you want. Take ownership of your mind and align with your authentic self. Otherwise, you automatically become someone else's idea of who you should be instead.

'This is how small and large groups of individuals become part of collective consciousness, without any thought to the agreement they are entering.'

When you connect with things you know to be wrong or incite hostility towards others, you get caught in a net where values, morals, and standards get violated. Remaining in a place where you must sacrifice yourself for acceptance into the tribe generally never ends well. Taking this route can be down to fear, shame, or resentment, and it can become tough to address the problems that accompany it. However, if you are willing and ready to become proactive, this will generate the dais necessary to overcome it.

To create an equilibrium to thrive, understand the pillars of life must be in balance: Cloé Madanes is a contemporary psychotherapist specialising in minimising interpersonal conflict. She helped develop the field of strategic intervention. She wrote.

"Everyone has basic needs, not merely desires but profound longings that underlie and motivate every choice you make. There are six basic needs everyone seeks to fulfil. (love and

connection, certainty, variety, growth, contribution, and significance.)"

These factors are essential for any individual to feel contentment and joy. The accomplishment you seek must be created from wholeness and not from a lifetime of limiting beliefs or self-sabotaging thoughts from the past. There isn't a career you cannot navigate effectively and efficiently at the highest levels, for when you build self-belief and self-worth in your aptitude, your desires obtain the potential to fly. Your new beginning can be just around the corner on the horizon; you will need to assume ownership for your choices, even if it doesn't work out the first time, and grow the courage to take a risk when you feel it's the right thing to do.

'If you try anything and it doesn't turn out as you thought, you can feel defeated in your head; if you allow this to take root, you will become defeated in life. Learn to separate the failure of a task from being a failure; the two are at opposing ends of the spectrum.'

Your self-talk enforces limited thinking and promotes your belief systems to produce what you see in the physical world. Making continuous, encouraging declarations to yourself through repetitive actions and positive affirmations produce new trains of thought and a victory mindset.

'Believing you can be a frontrunner guarantees success becomes predictable; it's all about perception.'

So, just this once, make the jump, take a chance, and see how far you can go. It's possible to have a designed life, and when you attain it, you can repeat the process to keep you there. With this change in awareness, your resilience can grow, making your future trials easier to navigate.

My pivotal moment came over a decade ago while working in food retail—a job I had held for more than twenty years. I was part of a wonderful work family who shared my life with me daily. We were a great team working together and enjoying the camaraderie; you could often hear the laughter echoing around the aisles from customers and staff, creating many moments, stories, and memories of a happy time.

'Positivity and humour are a big part of who I am, and I loved expressing that side of myself in my job. Even though I was not fully aware of it back then, I was beginning to uncover awareness of the person I wanted to represent.'

As the systems clerk for the store, I had to complete many reports daily. Although enjoyable for a time, the procedure became monotonous, and after six years in the job, I felt very restless and tired with the routine. I noticed on the canteen wall the company was recruiting for HR management trainees, which sparked my interest as I had never worked in that department before. I felt confident in my ability, as after two decades in various positions, including management. I had a wealth of knowledge I could use, so I decided to apply. There was just one small hurdle to overcome. The company insisted on a recommendation from the General Manager for entry into the course. I didn't see this as an issue as I felt I had a good relationship with mine.

'Sadly, it was not to be, and my request got shot down in flames. My manager compared me to a Fiat trying to be a Ferrari leaving me almost recoiling from the words, and then insulted me again by telling me I wasn't demure enough for the role anyway.'

At that moment, the wind gone from my sails; I was left questioning how I ever trusted this man to help me.

How did this societal ladder come to be, where those who hold positions above us decide whether we are worthy or not, based on their standards. There could never be a good enough reason for me to stay in a place that invested so little into its people. As the conversation unfolded, it became very apparent this man was devoid of the leadership skills required to see the drive and potential that was in me back then. I took myself away to a quiet space, my dreams of better crushed; there was no opportunity here or advancement on this path. The encouragement I was looking for would no longer be available to allow me to soar. The tears fell mainly from frustration; he never knew how I felt or the weight of regret I held in my heart for the years I had invested in the company.

'A change can happen for you at any moment, and due to my personal experience, I believe now it can. When the pain of settling where you are becomes so great, you will do whatever it takes to pursue an alternative. I now had no resistance to any substitute, and I became fully committed in the hunt for it.'

I had to work hard to prevent the words of that day seeping too deeply into my thoughts or damaging my self-esteem any further. This would be the turning point for a new life, a fork in the road where I would choose the opposite of everything I had been taught or expected to do, and I would find the courage to stay on track regardless of the consequences.

'I sat at my desk, pen in hand and wrote up my resignation letter. I was about to embark on an expedition, one that would take me places my imagination couldn't create a vision for at that time.'

I had no clue where I was going or what I was going to do. Yet, there was a part of me deep inside that knew I was here to find something better. Even though I enjoyed working with my colleagues, there was a void, a hole now, something I couldn't fill or put into words, but I longed to find out what it would be like on the outside, away from everything that was familiar.

It didn't happen overnight, and we struggled for some time, removing a full-time wage from our household. That said, my husband never complained or protested and continued to encourage me to pursue my new path.

I managed to secure a couple of additional positions, quickly, jobs were plenty then, so it didn't take long. First, was within a large national estate agency as a front-end sales assistant, and then in a manufacturing company ten months later. Both times I felt it was the answer, and the fresh start I had been yearning for. Unfortunately, it wouldn't take me long to discover I had made a huge mistake and realised I had traded one problem for another.

'Most days it felt like pushing a massive boulder up a hill. I got to the stage I hated waking up knowing I was going into those toxic spaces; I was starting to wonder if I would ever find a career that made me feel satisfied, significant or good enough.'

I never felt comfortable or supported by my managers in either of these posts. I tolerated disgusting behaviours from several staff members who were not happy about me being there. Even though I had changed career; I still didn't seem capable of effectively standing up for myself with the bullies. I was still emitting the wrong vibration as I hadn't altered my expectations or deservedness bar to demand better. I understand with hindsight how much those experiences mirrored my self-worth issues, giving me the necessary feedback I needed to realise it was never about anyone else. It was about me. I wouldn't have long to wait to be free of those restrictions, as the universe heard my anguish and it became a fleeting experience, releasing me through redundancy once again, due to the financial crisis of 2008.

'I have since learned everything that happened during that time was a universal nudge, begging me to stop applying for jobs as a crutch, to escape previous situations without altering who I was.'

This was my conditioning telling me I deserved nothing else, and unless I changed, it would keep giving me the same environment I was trying so hard to escape from. It did however, become my light bulb moment and with it a breakthrough. Around this time,

I began my personal development journey, which brought awareness of many things I hadn't understood before and helped me build my confidence. I realised it was my responsibility to become the standard for change and set a powerful example to attract the right people, career, and experiences to give me what I needed.

'Finding myself unemployed again and back in no man's land, pushed me to take a risk in an entirely different direction. This time I would create the skills necessary to work for myself. It was becoming crystal clear that having a boss wasn't working in my favour.'

So, I decided it was time to tap into my creative flair evident in my youth. My goal was to find a career of service where I could give back. I love being around people, and I managed to find something that ticked all the boxes. I enrolled in a local college course and retrained as a complementary and holistic therapist, expanding my practice with additional therapies over several years. I resurrected my diplomas in counselling and psychology that I gained in my twenties and used self-development material my husband gave me from his training as a Business Coach. This brought back my love of all things new, and I began investing heavily in those subjects again. I studied, listened, and read anything I could get my hands on about human behaviour and consumed videos and podcasts whenever I had spare time. I utilised all this material in my talking therapies along with physical treatments for any clients that wished it. This would generate all the information, data, and experiences necessary to spark my writing career and I can honestly say that since I did, I have never looked back.

'As crazy as this sounds, I have so much gratitude now for the man that told me no! Because of that key moment in my life, I became aware of how fiercely independent, capable, and strong, I really was.'

I now only had the desire and dream to follow my passion and help. I spent years honing my craft and learning new techniques I could share. The sense of involvement, satisfaction, and joy I felt daily was nothing I had ever felt before in any other career. I will feel gratitude for the rest of my life, that my clients felt safe enough to trust me with their personal stories. Those interactions and talks we shared were priceless to me; listening to their experiences and how it affected them, taught me so much about the human operating system and uncovered my purpose to produce the fuel I needed to push me continually. I had reached a tipping point where it became necessary to demand better for my life, the life of my family and all those who would cross my path from then on. I had learned one of life's most valuable lessons.

'I didn't have to be brilliant, flawless, or behave like anyone else; I just had to care.'

It has given me so many opportunities to learn amazing things, meet new people and express the gifts I was born with and never utilised. This has led me into a career I have developed a huge passion for. My wish is to share my findings and narrow the curve for those with a desire to do the same through my writing.

'You have a power inside; one you can use to change the way you think. Living unconsciously encourages negative beliefs and can leave you at the mercy of others you deem superior.'

Your belief systems from your past, are the very things that enable you to see this as factual. When you continue to listen to fear-based lies, it keeps you in a place that promotes silence, settling, accepting situations, feeling less, and mediocrity which can never offer you the opportunity to seek out your best.

'Living this way can restrict your right to be heard, for you may fear the end of a relationship, or worry you may lose your position or place in a company. You silence your voice to

protect yourselves from the anger of another, leaving you disempowered trying to protect your values and moral compass.'

Failing to step up, keeps a perpetual, cultural cycle in motion, where respect, honesty, integrity, and good manners get swept under the carpet again. Please don't wait as long as I did; let this be the sign you have been looking for and take the necessary action. The human condition can be eroded to the point of utter surrender, continuing to look outside yourself for solutions, leaves you beat by the sheer weight of it. You end up at the mercy of your circumstances, believing someone else is now responsible for saving you.

'So, you wait, moving further down the spiral sinking into abject defeat, failing to realise your inner power and natural ability to rise.'

It is essential you place learning at the forefront of what is important to you now; I cannot stress enough the breakthroughs you will find when choosing this path. You will discover many things, along with the means to identify your triggers, ones that push you into corners and convince you there is no escape. When you find out, many factors keep you in places of restriction; it can turn out to be the very thing to catapult you out of misery and towards freedom.

'I need you to be honest and open with yourself, peel away the layers and take a profound look inside, here you will uncover the reasons that drive you to engage in anything that brings you disharmony.'

There are going to be times you will continue to do things that hurt you, stay in careers that do not fulfil. You will tolerate imbalanced relationships, that are painful or abusive, often emotionally, mentally, and physically and lose yourself to be accepted by others.

'My inability to recognise how restricted I was, made me unconscious of my potential for over two decades, this placed me into a holding pattern, I had no awareness of how to get beyond, until I trained myself in the workings of the mind. There's always a cost, and frankly, it's too high.'

If you are miserable and refusing to change, you are ultimately choosing a life where you think you are less. You can never receive what was yours until you understand this. Handing your control over to another person and allowing them to make choices based on what is best for them, or what they deem to be best for you, will be the biggest error of your life. You are choosing this because you believe they have power over you. *Who do you think is responsible for that? Yes, it's YOU!*

Society is actively participating in the formation of a culture, in front and behind a computer screen. Ordinary people enduring awful situations at work and in life, it's time to find your voice and your worth, if your wish is to become strong enough to prevent any long-term damage. I know from experience you are far more likely to pull a friend or colleague from the ruins, so why then, do *'YOU'* stay in situations that require you to suspend **'YOUR'** values? Self-care must become your priority, this in time will deviate from your other disempowering programmes and become your new normal. Invest time in you, as it will remove those beliefs, that make you feel you need anything external to feel approval. You will know you were born enough.

'You are driving the vehicle that runs a continuous loop, constantly searching for the missing piece, the one you think you need to complete you; love is what is missing, and when you take the time to give it to yourself you will see what life has to show you.'

No one is the ultimate guru or can fix your troubles, just at the right moment when everything is falling in around you. When you exercise due diligence first, you educate yourself in the best way possible, you reclaim dominion of your thoughts and remain the victor, removing any wish to be the injured party.

Realise this, each of you can be your own guru by trusting your inner voice. You have the answers, and your intuition never steers you wrong, for it alerts you to any discord or gives a warning before entering an uneasy relationship or a questionable business deal.

'Are you guilty of entertaining negative emotions, like shame, blame, worry, anxiety, envy, depression and resentment? Are you frightened to show the world who you are? Do you fear rejection, and think you won't be accepted or loved, if people see the real you?'

Learn to free yourself from these crippling states by getting out of your own way. You must become your leading authority, this engages a powerful machine (*your mind*), and when infused with the right message, it will only accept the best future for you, and that includes uncovering your authentic self.

'At the core of dissonance lies fear, everyone is fearful of something, born of unconscious patterns you learnt from others throughout your lifetime. I never understood the idea of entertaining stuff full of worry, offering nothing but misery to the recipient, as it took so much of their power away. Especially when the alternative would have required the same focus, yet they never chose that path.'

Discovering those who have witnessed the same pain as you, enables understanding, and a place to connect at a deep level. You are not alone or the only one going through tests, if you are to free yourself from constraints, you must be ready to step up your game every day and be encouraged to know there is always support when you choose to utilise it. Please find a way to display your courage as it sets an action in motion to raise your standards to demand better. Once you reach this place, in time, it will inevitably begin to send a clear sign out into the world. The vibration you will now emit will be one of strength, sending a robust signal to others of what you will tolerate and anything that will undoubtedly become unbearable. When you raise the bar for your life, you elevate your experience to a whole new level, and this cultivates a new truth, where you will be unwilling to sink into conformity like so many others. Instead, you will see the advantages of fulfilling your true potential. The benefits achieved through change to the self are crucial for real transformation. The bonus you will receive from this quest is the impact on your behaviours, actions, feelings, and ultimately the connections you make with others.

'When you adopt this behaviour, it harvests an optimistic, confident demeanour and others will gravitate towards you naturally. It's infectious, contagious, and addictive. Those who elicit these qualities are easily identified, as it radiates

from them like a powerful energy. Wouldn't you like to be one of them?'

Those who operate from this podium will always get more done; these individuals have learned the laws of life and are more effective in their chosen fields. They understand the power of a progressive attitude and how the application of it constitutes change. The person responsible for stopping your growth is *YOU*. You only ever get what you believe, or what you feel in your heart you deserve.

'Any contradiction to this is always via ideologies based on fears from the past; unfortunately, without new knowledge, you will wonder why what you genuinely want never shows up.'

The course of your life can alter when you learn how to access this higher power. You can amend the beliefs you seem so intent on protecting, and I will teach you in chapter four, *The Science Behind your Thoughts*, how to rethink what is currently controlling those feelings, and show you they are nothing but untruths that stop your elevation. As you travel along this enlightenment journey, it will be necessary to connect to internal nudges you feel.

This is your sign (*your intuition*), giving the green light calling you towards an alternative path and encouraging you to develop the skills to accept this as your new truth. Then and only then will you stop fighting your habitual will.

'The way is now clear to move beyond automatic patterns and restrictions, as you will soon learn and understand most of them, were set by an external source.'

The ground can now literally shift below your feet, for real change evolves through a person's self-education and is encouraged by those who surround and support those changes. This is the ingredients required for the motivation to keep going; those forward-thinking emotions will propel you headfirst into better than you anticipated, or what you were fearful of leaving behind.

'Negative behaviours, circumstances, situations, or beliefs that allow too much external force to penetrate thoughts can and will subsequently alter how you feel about yourself. Examples of these states might be an overbearing boss, an abusive relationship, the loss of something important, a diagnosis or an event that creates an upsetting emotional connection to that time.'

When you reach a state of conscious awareness, you will know regardless of how you feel; you are responsible for how you act. It is always your response to any situation that ultimately fuels the conflict, due to your emotional attachment to the problem, person, or event. True liberation comes from awareness of behaviours and responsibility for failings; this is how you grow tenacity. You have the authority to choose for yourself to use that grit and love your story or spend the rest of your life hustling for your worthiness.

'Stop doing the same things over and over expecting something different. Inspire yourself with new learnings that offer answers, and let it drive you towards a healthier destination.'

I often wish people could understand my perspective as a therapist; If you could see yourself through my eyes, you would know how precious you are, and never waste another moment measuring yourselves against others. So much is fabricated and inaccurate anyway. Placing too much interest on those who appear to have more only drives you back into lack and envy. It's the very thing if you give it enough traction, will leave you feeling like a failure and frankly it's insane at best. You all have your lives to live, not one based on another's experience; everyone is different, so your paths must be too.

'This interpretation of life is only a tiny snapshot of something so much bigger you can't see.'

The social media circus has run away with rational thinking, watching from behind a screen analysing how incredible the lives of others appear to be, is moderately disturbing. This is a contributory factor to the state of the mental health and self-worth issues happening today. Regularly engaging in these platforms without a healthy perspective is fuelling the problem. Those compelled to hide behind things to impress, gain attention, and attract followers or likes are often not rooted in authenticity. Real-life consists of meaningful things you interact with daily. Spending time with colleagues who include you and give purpose—sharing dinner with your partner or family and discussing the events of your day while you were apart. Getting on the floor and playing with your children or snuggling up for a bedtime story. It's hanging out with your mates and laughing so hard you want those feelings to last forever; it's those impulsive little things that make up a beautiful life. The virtual world is becoming the optical prism to view your worth. If you can't survive for periods without your phone fused to your palm, then you have replaced fantasy with reality. It won't take long to erode those connections, for when you get around to noticing your company, there may be nothing to greet you but an empty chair.

'It's a heart-breaking reminder when life teaches you painful lessons from your choices. Awareness should give you the jolt

required to correct your course, even if they are the hardest ones to swallow.'

This is the universal nudge I was speaking about earlier and can show you the path to your bliss or place signs in your way to alert you to damaging actions. Choose to **RISE** higher every day and prepare to disconnect and appreciate the finer things in life. Giving attention you can never get back on something that offers little return is not the best use of your time. Embrace the moment you are in now and let go of everything else. You live in a great timeline with new and exciting developments, and It's natural to want to be a part of it all. I know I have been mesmerised by its lure and it's easy for time to run away with you when you start. So, to gain control of my days, I schedule a little time online in the morning and evening to post things relevant to my business and life. I potter around for a bit and catch up with posts from friends that interest me.

'I have, in reflection, found the best experiences are those where I am physically with people. I love conversations with friends, travel, a theatre, or a movie show, or walking in nature without my phone. I am old enough to remember what life was like when there was no such thing as a mobile or cell, and if you needed to call someone, you were tethered to the unit by a cord on the wall.'

Such memories reminded me of when it seemed easier to focus, without the constant pings from a phone as a distraction. I'm a realist, and I know things can never go back to how they were as technology is a way of life now. It has opened remarkable doors I might never have found and connected me with people all over the world. I hope though; everyone can find joy away from the screens that leave them hypnotised by unattainable standards and get engaged by connection again.

'If you can cultivate perspective and not get drawn into the madness of it all, it won't have such a devastating impact on your self-worth. Use it to build a business, stay in touch with friends and family, create fantastic content or encourage others to educate themselves through those messages.'

Remember, if you are using these platforms to grow a brand, a business or make yourself more visible. You will have to develop a thicker skin, for the higher you rise, the more vocal your opponents and trolls will become, and you need to be mentally ready for that. Therefore, it becomes vital to believe others do not measure your worth only you do. So much of your lives will be communicated through these online portals moving forward.

Hence, as I indicated earlier, get balance, prioritise physical connections and remove people who target or discredit you in any way. Stay alert and if all else fails, refuse to read the negative stuff on your feed or block anyone who pedals it. ***Do not Engage!***

When you decide on better, your standards rise and form new habits. This guarantees your interactions will be a more positive and constructive experience. With your new outlook, you can train your emotional intelligence to supersede everything else. You must control your mood and prohibit any damaging behaviours from others who actively encourage bigoted views or prejudice. These ideologies come from the limited thinking conditioned mind, one that does not know how to accept others just as they are.

'Those who spend their time in attack mode view others with judgement. They have been taught this somewhere along the line, so allowing their behaviour to affect how you feel, when they have nothing to pull from themselves is pointless. When you give their words no power, they fall away.'

Be mindful of who you share personal things with too, because it is nothing more than fuel for gossip, even more so if they envy who you are, or what you are trying to achieve. This ensures you give attention and effort to those who deserve your time. You can now get on with living. Invest in your growth and reject such things if they enter your domain in the future.

'By doing so, you elevate yourself from this contagion and dry up the gene pool they seem so intent on attacking. If there is no fodder, there is no fight.'

You can release these emotions if you have been on the receiving end and eliminate its energy by forgiving those who delivered it. This does not condone poor behaviour but releases the emotive stranglehold it has on you. Those undesirable situations that arise throughout your life, must become the ones to occupy the least amount of your time. Staying locked in never-ending cycles of over-analysis, encourages you to give up your power to those you deem stronger or who intimidate you the most. Talking and thinking about it consumes your mind and lowers your internal vibration, leaving you disturbed, depleted, unhappy or angry. When you can see it from this angle, you are responsible for cultivating the amount of harm it causes you or the amount of time you choose to keep it in your awareness and give it attention. Eventually, like the domino effect, when values get disrupted, you behave very differently and transmit those feelings to those in your closest circle.

Your need to continually vent generates a repetitive pattern and trains your brain to believe the subject is of immense interest to you, keeping it unconsciously alive. This unending sequence of uneasiness will remain until you learn to let it go wholly from your awareness. If you don't months or decades later, you will still believe it is the reason for the way you conduct yourself now.

'Allowing anyone to limit your life and make you feel less than you know you are, is a waste of your days, how much of it impacts your thought patterns with reverence to your value, can have catastrophic consequences for your future.'

Choosing to maintain painful memories in your present reality is how you extend your refractory period, (*the amount of time you allow a situation, person, or event to hinder your life*). It will stay there for as long as it takes to realise it's ok to let it go. When you give anyone too much space inside your head, they will become your jailer, causing you to stay in a place you were never destined for.

'Everyone has memories from the past that have caused them pain; it can either define you or give you the fuel to change and choose who you want to become.'

Regardless of what you had to wade through, the lesson within can equip you for what lies ahead on the journey. Your ability to realise just how far you have come and overcome recalibrates the route to a brighter horizon and brand-new destinations. Every day you make selections and take actions to support those choices. Who you surround yourself with daily are contributing to your beliefs regardless of whether you are consciously aware of it or not?

'What environment are you choosing to live in, whose voices are you listening to, are they helping you rise or pulling you down to a level they prefer to operate on?'

You become influenced by those you spend time around, and they reinforce your thoughts due to similar patterns woven within those unions. Look at your life right now, who are your biggest influencers? Do they encourage and openly celebrate your achievements, or are you actively hiding things to avoid confrontation? Have you reached a point where you prefer to stay in the back blindly following the herd with little disparity? You choose, so, reassess your life and those you give your time and attention to.

'If you are always fighting against an invisible force with no end in sight, are you sure you want to spend more time forcing your way through that?'

If you identify yourself here and it has tripped a switch internally, one that disrupts you so deeply, you have the greatest desire to grow from this place. Then take the time, follow the nudge, and start introducing unfamiliar things into your day that push you beyond comfort. If I have stirred your imagination, then get ready to feel considerable resistance. You will have to be brave and build tenacity along with an impenetrable barrier to repel those intent on seeing you fail. You must love yourself first to make available what you need to feel whole, then send love and forgiveness to the people who do not recognise the value of your journey. It's time for you now to emulate the core of the best people, those who made a conscious choice daily to climb above any tests. I learnt these lessons from others, and with immeasurable gratitude for all it revealed, I pass it on to you now.

The emergence of what follows is your chance to soar to new heights. Your knowing will let go of what stops you so you can climb forever......

Geraldine Mair

- CHAPTER THREE -

STEPPING INTO GREATNESS

QUOTE

'Once you make your mind up there is no reason for you to be average, you are beginning to understand the capacity you have for greatness, step out of your comfort zone and into your destiny.'

Geraldine Mair

During my youth, I always thought success was an elusive thing that belonged to wealthy individuals or celebrities from affluent backgrounds. I later discovered my programming of this concept is called conditioned reinforcers. The first comes from what surrounds you in your environment during childhood; the second is a process where similar messages and stimuli later in life get paired with primary reinforcers to strengthen those behaviours and beliefs.

'This is how it was so difficult for me to comprehend that I could have enough potential to override these thoughts or have the capability to become like those I admired so much.'

When I discovered personal development, it taught me to change my internal dialogue. With consistent study, I uncovered many things and got excited at how my life could change through the implementation of my new-found knowledge. This awareness would help me to understand that others with similar backgrounds had pitched their tent in the same camp, oblivious of the personal cost or impact it would have on their lives.

The environment I lived in back then didn't provide me with any evidence you could be wealthy and generous at the same time. It always had negative connotations attached to it. Many individuals around me often vocalised negativity towards anyone who earned enough to make them very wealthy. The beneficiaries of this lifestyle had to be corrupt or dishonest to align with their beliefs and make sense of how unjust it was. Because of what I heard, it became my truth too.

'Separation in society is born from ignorance, situations where the back story is unknown, so the gaps get filled with a variety of sources, none that have any basis in fact. This behaviour encourages beliefs to make you think you are correct; you require this to resonate with your internal coding, and it is responsible for breeding dislike towards those who have what you don't.

After spending many years learning about habit patterns, I know money isn't a bad thing; it's simply energy, a symbol used in the transfer of a service or product. There is nothing evil about money, nor has there ever been, only the thoughts and beliefs attached to it make it so. If you want to make a difference, you must accept it as a requirement of life and stop being fearful of it.

'My continuous education has given me the ability to expand those rigid ideas with a brand-new perspective. I now understand there are many wealthy people in the world, who are active philanthropists, giving in wonderful ways every day of their lives. To do the same, I must too build a mindset to contribute at a higher level and give to others in a way that enhances both.'

I should mention that wealth comes in many guises and is not only measured in monetary terms as so many choose to believe. You can have a modest life with an abundance of friends and family, hobbies you love and a humble home that feels like a palace to you and still feel like the wealthiest person alive. It becomes a personal measure of what you need to feel whole. I hope this helps to demonstrate an alternative path to question things in your life that cause you to feel dislike towards others, regardless of the reason. I don't want you to be kept back by false beliefs or add any more years to your personal punishment term. Life can be so much more when you stop believing there is nothing better for you in the future, there is, and I can show you how to find it. The most critical part of this process will be your ability to elevate your self -love, belief, and acceptance of others, regardless of what they have or where they are on the journey. When you combine this with enough proficiency at employing what you learn, everything changes for the better. Otherwise, it becomes nothing more than words on a page.

'I offer you this gift by showing you the power of your human mind. Let me show you how to love your life and walk you through the maze to erase repeat patterns. You will come to learn it is nothing more than a selection of paradigms, built around a fear mentality that keeps you trapped.

Your comfort zone, a place most are choosing to live, is only a set of conditioned responses, of habits to keep you within the familiar. The more you participate in these rituals, the more embedded in your subconscious they become. You will feel safe there, but you will not grow; you will consign yourself into a place and become unable to stretch your mind to aspire for better or higher. You will accept this is your life; it is nothing more than what you have become habituated by.

'YOU WERE TAUGHT THIS REMEMBER THAT!'

What about wanting the desires of your heart? Instead of accepting a familiarised stance marinated over countless years. Recognition and awareness starts a whole new process of actions to modify thought patterns. You will reach a tipping point when you perform it often enough, and your future reality will look entirely different from the one you are currently living in now.

'There was a poll taken in America, referenced by Earl Nightingale on his video titled "The Strangest Secret", Recorded in the 1950s', yet so far ahead of its time. Earl articulates how the collective mentality works and keeps people in repetitive cycles.'

Earl states most people act like everyone else, without considering why. The most alarming thing is, they are replicating ninety-five per cent of people, who continue to follow pre-programmed expectations and end up in the vast majority who leave destiny to chance.

Why do you conform?

Because most people believe external circumstances beyond their control shape life. A herding mentality encompassing millions who abide by societal patterns inherited from parents, teachers, and peers. An endless sequence of generations echoing the same programmed path, unaware of any alternative. Let's ponder over the recorded statistics for those who succeeded based on Earl's findings. If ninety-five per cent of people chose to conform and follow the crowd, only five per cent of that poll opted for a completely different route; the option that offered them a life they wanted.

'Hanging around with people who have no independent thought, can only return a similar version of life for you, as you become programmed by what you surround yourself with. This behaviour ensures you will never be any different from the most significant per cent, like Earl's study.'

You are following an automatic code, just like everyone else. The evidence I collected even within this current timeline confirms many people still do this without question and remain disillusioned by life. Those individuals go to work each day and are miserable being there, they choose to give away many hours daily to make a wage, yet they do not use any free time to create a better future. If they thought about it, it's a chance to learn new things or use transferable skills to find an alternative. They might even feel inspired and stimulated to take part in fulfilling contribution again, and their lives could look vastly different.

'Understand when you are unhappy, you unconsciously affect those you interact with because your disharmony filters through, which can manifest as envy, anger, impatience, or annoyance. When out of balance, you cause tension within the units you frequent.'

In my story, I had to do the internal work to break long term patterns that hampered my progress and rediscover potential I had forgotten was in there. By altering my course through self-education, I have embarked on an evolutionary journey with the grit to demand better.

'Your fear of the unknown is the only thing holding you captive at every turn; the distress of perceived failure keeps

you rooted in mediocrity and just getting by. Convincing yourself, you do not have the capability or deservedness for anything else.'

Through reading my truth, you can see the opportunity of a pivotal moment, and take the chance to act on it. Question what you choose to believe, find your courage when the door opens and just step through.

'The only way to provide you with the best path now will be the one less travelled.'

Many who ventured onto this path faced innumerable challenges, but it never stopped them. Even when money was tight or things didn't happen at the speed they needed, their belief in their dream never diminished. They choose instead to continuously work on their resilience, to rise and try again. Those brave enough to step into leading roles, stay on track and fight for what they believe, can expect to see their thoughts manifest into form.

'When you have this amount of mental fortitude and self-belief, irrespective of the knocks, you can end up in the five per cent who manufacture their life by design.'

Will *You* fall when you take this route? At some point, most likely, for determination is built from trials and never during the easy times. Remember, though, even if you end up on your knees, as long as you get back up, you are still a winner.'

'Get ready to climb your mountains and face the things that will cross your path, look upon your endeavours as lessons and teachers, and you anchor within you the very technique used by others to pave the way to reach your greatness.'

Your life can now reflect that which you desire when you are not afraid to fail in the pursuit of your biggest successes. I have uncovered that only through the countenance of those gifts, regardless of the risks, I feel truly alive and living my purpose. It is a spectacular place to live every day, and I enjoy embracing the opportunities that appear on my trail with enthusiasm, revealing treasures destined only for me.

'Greatness is your birthright, and with it a stage to explore your gifts and talents, the ones you brought into this world to express in abundance.'

Each day can be different, a joy, a pleasure, living in the moment, removes any fear or need for control. You will not require anything beyond this to feel complete, for you will know deep inside, you have nothing to prove, and life is better when it's lived this way.

Your inbuilt survival mechanism keeps you within a framework you recognise, restricting and repressing ideas that deep down, you know in your heart to be good. Let that voice in and make it louder than your nemesis; *(your negative self-talk)* and you can now answer those universal nudges when they show up. I promise you what happens after this will surprise you.   You have potential to add to the whole in some way, so stop randomly following patterns from others or trying *to* copy what they're doing, without really questioning the end goal, as surely this must be a pointless exercise for you now?'

'Your life's work will indeed take up a large portion of your time here, so make sure it's something you want to get out of your bed for.'

Your purpose is towards expansion by learning new things, when this triggers that dormant part of you it will ultimately drive you to want more. Your measure of greatness will become evident by your ability to convey integrity, love, and kindness for your fellow man. Unity and connection are your source, yet some choose to operate within mindsets fixed on polarity, rivalry, and disagreement. Look at your life? Are you functioning like this?

'This is egotistical behaviour, driven by a need to be right, popular, smug, arrogant, better or something else. Or perhaps reflects a sense of lack in you, or an inability to achieve anything worthwhile yourself, perpetuating the need to tear down those around you.'

If so, this is a familiar reaction you have learned, compelling you to find significance because you think you are less.

'Your desire to push down everyone else in the pursuit of anything is the measure of a coward and is not integral to your source. You are designed to want the best for yourself, and this should lead you to thoughts of wanting the best for others.'

It is persistent belief patterns that are guilty of fostering repetitive, harmful, behaviours. You cannot support someone out front if you are always talking about them when they are not around. Trying to justify those actions inside a pool of individuals who have nothing to offer, will keep you chained to harmful habits. It's important to be proud of those around you, who dare to do something different.

'My admiration will always go to the brave souls that never settled but charged head-on into the test, despite the naysayers, haters and outside noise that hunted them down on the way there.'

Everything you get to enjoy daily has come from the imagination of another, their innovative thoughts have made your life in this timeline remarkable, and yet some seem incapable of acknowledging it, more so if it happens to be produced by someone familiar. I have written this book on a computer, something I could not have done in my youth as it was not available to me back then, and this is only one invention of many to enhance the living experience.

'A mind that believes in possibility has limitless options; therefore, you should always try to support those bold enough to carry their dreams through to completion, in the end, you have no idea how it might evolve or what will transpire.'

Never let the lack of support from anyone deter your ability to climb into a vision of better. Anyone who discredits you does not grasp the universal laws, for if they did, they would comprehend how it erodes the values of the person whose ideas they are refuting, and their self-worth along with it.

If you are culpable of partaking in these acts trusting it's the only way to gain popularity, then you are delusional, it's the worst kind there is, for by your deception and insincere acts you are wounding both parties. Is this really who you want to be, or represent to the world?

No one who participates in these acts has a desire to be on the receiving end of this appalling behaviour. Stop! Listen to your heart and start working towards a version of yourself; you can be proud to be around.

'This toxic pond reiterates and fortifies belief patterns that steal any potential, regardless of how much you want it. Only when someone else makes you aware you are off track; it becomes crystal clear by just how much you have neglected your values.'

How wonderful is it to celebrate something achieved in your life, and a tribe ready to crack the champagne open with you? From this point on commit to becoming your friends, family, and colleagues' biggest fan and those flood gates of support can overflow into your own life.

'Feeling appreciated for your work and the effort that went into it is amazing, your self-confidence and self-worth are automatically raised, along with deep feelings of gratitude.'

You were born to live this way, to love, to accept and to encourage. If you are unfortunate enough to have found yourself in a group who ignore, disrespect, or openly discourage your journey, then what are you doing? And what are you gaining from growing these connections?

'No one should have to filter their wins to feel included or understood. Playing small serves no one and if the relevant conduct you deserve is not forthcoming, may I suggest the only thing you need to change will ultimately be YOU and what you are choosing to tolerate!'

Refuse to participate and start helping; instead, you can't change other people, and it's not your job anyway. Your responsibility for your life is to learn and expect better. It has been there all along just waiting for you to grab hold of.

'When you rise tomorrow, and you see your reflection in the mirror, I want you to tell yourself you will no longer be dulling your shine, from now on your aim will be to polish it daily, making it so vivid it sparkles like a diamond.'

You have a large reserve tank, and a mental toughness available when you stop faking it, so, start living large and with intention. Every one of you can do much more than you think you can, by pushing those boundaries regularly, it will surprise you just how easy it can be to get out of the tedious routine.

The decision to become willing and committed to the process will prove what you can get done and trust me, don't be surprised if you discover a hidden gem that's been in there for years. Forgive those who attack, belittle, and show disdain for anything that contradicts what they believe. Stand in your power, for no one can hurt you when you know you are enough. Disliking anyone for a perceived difference is always wrong; no one is born this way. It happens through the conditioning of those who never learnt to cut old cords, remaining unconscious; instead; this is how patterns are passed on and encouraged to continue. This mentality is such a narrow one.

'When you believe a great life is destined only for the few, that abundance is scarce, and if everyone ascends, it depletes the resources, you will never have the life you want. You must learn to silence that noise from your reality. Abundance means plenty, and you live in a world overflowing with it, in all things, don't measure it in only financial gains.'

Think about the abundance of nature, of air you breathe, water in the oceans, food in the stores, the love for your partners and children, the love for yourself, the potentials available when you believe in the power of your fertile mind.

Most adults don't know what it's like to love life fully for who they are and what they have, choosing instead to give focus to what they perceive is missing. Through the transformation of old wounds, you find your way back to self-love, and a clearer vision of the blessings already in your life, ensuring each day that passes from now offers more fulfilment and freedom for those who choose it.

'You have the fire on the inside everyone does, it's time to learn how to set it free and keep it ablaze with energy forever, you can change your story and supersede those tough encounters on your journey.'

Now is your time to develop the greatness you were born into this world to express. Ignore the critics and place that available energy and attention into your **"A"** game, and nothing can penetrate that tough exterior, ensuring your altitude in this lifetime is assured.

'You are a miraculous creation; the likes of which will never pass through this way again. The synchronicities that had to take place for you to even exist in this timeline are extraordinary. Like snowflakes, every single human being is unique, rare, and magnificent, and that includes YOU!'

Any threat can only persist if you permit those negative thoughts into your mind; this inadvertently creates the networks in your brain, encouraging you to quit your voyage, the one you were ready and willing to navigate. Electing to pass your baton to outside stimuli, reinforces those false views.

'Re-read the last two paragraphs as many times as you need until you emotionally connect to the message. I hope this awakens what is hidden just below the surface that you could not see, or the beliefs you cultivated that blinded you to it. That shadow impeding your growth will never be anything outside of you; this is an internal predator.'

Stop settling for situations where others govern your course or believing you don't deserve to have your fair share. Your role within this contract amounts to nothing positive. With no return on your investment, it will only construct a barrier so high it will destroy any chance you have for elevation. Commit to choosing actions and people that inspire you, and have a beneficial influence to reach for more, do more and become more through that positive example. *You do your best when your aim is beyond your own measurement.*

'Your visions can manifest and come into clear focus with massive action, you will never find the answers on the outside so stop looking, for only those who understand the workings of the mind truly awaken.'

When it remains buried, it offers you nothing than a missed opportunity to free potential. Your self-imposed fears and internal beliefs will keep you in those fated positions forever, until you get to the point you won't accept it anymore. Never let fear hold you back, for gaining the ability to defeat those things uncovers a winner.

'When you act out of fear, shame, resentment, or regret for anything you are expressing a pain in you, either current or historic, and it can generate damaging sparks, you will feel continually. Now you are fostering unpleasant and hurtful emotions that are destructive to the self.'

Try infusing your life with self-love from a current awareness instead. This will flood you with inner joy and power, delivering a productive consequence for your life. The most significant gift you can ever award yourself is the capacity to enjoy every moment. When you live in the present, you embrace your bliss with no desire to change the past or predict the future.

'Start building bridges towards what you want and stop trying to scale social ladders to impress or be accepted.'

In over ten years of studying this material, I now enjoy a calm, content life. I never sweat the small stuff, instead choosing to direct focus and consideration into gratitude for what I do have. From this position, I source solutions when I encounter a bump in the road whilst navigating my path. I urge you to keep reading the passages in the additional volumes that support this book as it will offer you an obvious sign of where you need to modify your perspectives.

'When you gain a better awareness of your beliefs, you will understand how it can enlarge your problems or give you infinite possibilities towards solutions; it depends on how you allow yourself to see it.'

Transformation is painful and hours get wasted looking for reasons not to follow those signs. It is normal to feel a certain amount of safety in comfort, yet it can prevent you from releasing your flair. Find the strength to follow any enterprise you believe to be worthy of your time, and freely express those desires with inspired, nonstop action.

'A different experience is waiting for you here as soon as you decide it's time, you must find this path to change your mind and step away from all that is familiar. When you follow that leading voice, the warrior in you can invite it in when you are ready and open to receive it.'

Now you have the first steps towards understanding how to take your life in a different direction, one that may have intimidated you before or that you never took the time to consider. You are not stuck, you are loyal to forms of behaviour, which brought you to this place, and are now more harmful than helpful. It is your will that fights those dreams and keeps them hidden from your experience.

'You do yourself a massive disservice by refusing to respond; you repress your aptitude of discovery into new areas, new people, new opportunities and encounters, the world also misses out on those special abilities you are failing to use or actively share.'

You need to become your priority, self-care is one of the most underutilised facets in a person's life, and yet your ability to perform at optimal levels is impossible on an empty tank. You must learn this and apply it, for the impact you can have on yourself and others when you invest this way can be immense.

'When you know you are here to contribute, living from your truth becomes as important as breathing'.

Your progress is impossible without change, for it is you, and only you, who can make those alterations. The critical difference between seeing any adaption to life as a coping mechanism. *(doing it because you feel you must)* and embracing that change to win are poles apart. Do not be afraid of what you will find or uncover within these pages; you have invested time into reading this information, so, push aside fear and get ready to own it, embrace it, and follow it. This is the truth of life and the information you need to propel you forward.

'Inside of you is a powerful instrument, your very own GPS and it can tell when you're off track, or something just feels wrong. By refusing to listen or take the right action, you tell your subconscious to remain in stalemate, and it's always listening. It's time to silence negative input and open your ears to a more positive internal dialogue.'

This force is searching for a way out, it lives within and wants the absolute best for you, so wipe the slate clean and begin again, daily if required, and you can access an ocean of possibility, and that changes everything. Waste not a minute more of your valuable time in the pursuit of anything that does not bring you joy. The delight you find in anything that raises your emotions and makes you smile is a feeling stirring inside, looking for an open window to free itself, and this is your purpose showing you the way. If you can find a means to harness that authority and use it to make a living by sharing it with the world, you may just have found your very own nirvana. So, where do you start? By exploring avenues towards an alternative, you may not be able to give up your day job. However, you can still find experiences during your transition that can help you. When I worked in retail, I knew deep down it wasn't my calling.

'However, I have always been a happy, positive person, and I found a way to make it enjoyable. My passion is helping people, and I took every opportunity to interact with staff and customers in ways I could express it. I got to know people very well over the years and built trust within those units to encourage strong bonds to grow. My day-to-day tasks might not have been the most fulfilling at the time, but harnessing aspects of my personality and utilising them in ways that brought me joy, got me through the days with much less mental effort.'

You can adopt this strategy too; everyone has a talent or a gift, don't bury it under years of despair, instead think about how you can help make your environment better until you get an opportunity to change it. Harness any free time to investigate the career market and get yourself out there again. I love the saying *'if you're not in it you can't win it.'* And this is more relevant than ever in this process.

'Please don't take jobs out of desperation, without giving too much thought to the consequences of that action. Look at how many errors I made until I listened to my gut. For, it often becomes evident further down the line; your choices are what you are conditioned to expect, they are usually short-lived, not the best, or anywhere close to what you genuinely wanted.'

It is always a two-way street when you make conscious choices about your future and where you invest your time. So, if you are willing to take the jump, be patient and get the right fit to deliver at least seventy-five per cent of your non-negotiables. This gives you the best chance of moving to something that offers a lot more than staying where you are. When you are content with your decision and have fewer objections for your mind to contend with, this will reassure you moving was right. If you choose to work for yourself and start a company, using an idea or skill, this will take the most courage and the most significant risk. I have personally discovered it has been the greatest decision with the finest rewards. For liberation inevitably comes when you take total control of your destiny and every decision after that.

'Give yourself the brush to become the artist, the instrument to become the musician and the opportunities to secure the leading role of your movie. Now you know what it will take to get there, you need to remove your fears, the poor inner self-talk and any input from others preventing you from taking the reins.'

Those who shared their stories of disappointment with me, clarified my findings, that any negative influence, whether from themselves or others caused them to terminate their climb.

'Never settle, instead fill your thoughts with abundance for your life, one you frequently visualise in your mind that drives every fibre within you, and then get to work!'

Whatever route you take, do it with integrity and belief, and what you desire can come into form.

'Clients I knew who made the jump, expressed how it brought back thirst for life, saved marriages, delivered excellent financial results when they needed it the most and allowed them to live life by design. There are many happy endings when you decide to step into your greatness.'

The shift takes place only when you place yourself at the helm, do the work to reprogramme unhelpful beliefs and refuse to forfeit those new learnings. Now you are acting constructively towards an evolved destination, and not via the agendas of someone else. Be ready to get your climbing boots on and get into training.

Nothing will change if your life is unhappy until you put in the time required to alter that trajectory. Keep in mind if you are looking for convenient, you will only do the minimum necessary, and there will be no advancements. You will continue to slip back down to the foothills to start the climb again, a lot of people are guilty of this, without understanding their behaviours keep this cycle going.

'You must learn the rules of science and how your brain operates to alter that course. When you understand the power of commitment over convenience, you will do whatever it takes to get you there.'

Real change can only become a habit when you repeat the process many, many times. This is how your brain recognises the creation of a new file. When enough time has passed for the latest software to be installed; you will be able to complete the task with a lot less effort. By committing to this process, you must do whatever it takes, even if it involves a whole lot of discomfort and pain in the process.

Push on and push through, with everything you have, even if you fail a few times or are disappointed by the results. Success is rarely achieved with the first attempt; the rewards for persistence lie on the other side of this barrier.

'There is no substitute to this method, for change in all its forms, often comes with mental and emotional pain, however, for those willing to take on the mission, it is always worth the effort it will take to get you there.'

A human being can undergo extraordinary mental, emotional, and physical tests and still rise victorious, for nothing can impede a person with the right mental attitude. You develop resilience through experiences, and this is how you learn endurance.

'When facing those tests, you often need to conquer the enemy inside that convinces you to quit. You can have power and strength over your mind, and when you believe this, your need for practically anything will be made available.'

When it's over, it will never be the problem you won against, but your internal voice. Discovering the valour to go on regardless of the trials will take you beyond any impasse and set you firmly on a higher path. The best reference I can find for this endurance level is in *"Man's Search for Meaning"* by Victor. E. Frankl and if you haven't read it, I encourage you to do so. He was an Austrian neurologist and psychiatrist, a prisoner in the concentration camps in Auschwitz and one of the most documented holocaust survivors.

'His captors tried to break his mind and body, and for years he endured the most horrific conditions. Yet somehow this man was able to harness every ounce of perseverance and tolerance needed to build the mental fortitude for survival.'

It took him beyond his experience and on to a vision of a future far larger than any exterior burden placed upon him. One of the most profound quotes from his book resonates with everything I have learned on this journey so far.

"When we are no longer able to change a situation, we are challenged to change ourselves. Everything can be taken from a man but one thing: the last of the human freedoms. To choose one's attitude in any given set of circumstances is to choose one's own way."

Victor E Frankl

Take strength from those who have conquered and risen stronger, and seek to emulate their mental capacity for toughness. You will never have to endure this man's level of pain, but like him, you can be the master of your mind, the captain of your ship, only rendered off course, when *you* allow other people or events to permeate your thoughts, ones that make you question you're '*Why*'. For no impediment can prevent you from reaching your peak, except the ones you continue to pollute your own thoughts with. Self-discipline begins with the mastery of those internal thoughts. When you have no awareness of those feelings, you become powerless and will continue to be led by a set of programmes that manage your behaviours.

That mind of yours is a beautiful piece of equipment capable of offering you an amazing life. Refuse to be a slave to habitual programming and instead use this information to become its master, and you grow to be infinite.

Note: You can find over two hundred strategies in the additional volumes that accompany this book. They will teach you how to harness your power, alter perspective and answer questions to help you find your right path.

'Refuse to be held back by anything and use this information to step into your greatness.

Start today the world is waiting…'

- CHAPTER FOUR -

THE SCIENCE BEHIND YOUR THOUGHTS

QUOTE

'The negative influences you are witness to every single day can fall away from your experience when you refuse to exercise or engage in the behaviours that generate any awareness of them.'

Geraldine Mair

Welcome to the science behind your thoughts. This will help you detangle the myths around your beliefs and unravel your paradigms, to encourage you to reach for the exceptional. After years of studying the mind, and looking into how human beings operate, I have a clearer understanding of why you do what you do. When you learn this material, you will develop the aptitude to adjust your course when life catches you on the blindside.

'No change can ever take place when you settle for the circumstances around you, for when you do, you accept you are less. The immensity of your mind, your thoughts, beliefs, and software design, have created the connections necessary to place limiting beliefs on your life. Unconsciously injecting the fuel required to lay the foundations that shaped you; it is responsible for the experiences you will be witness to during your natural life here.'

These patterns govern the choices you make and the amount of risk you will consider towards a preferred objective. Living like this makes it difficult to set a goal in the first place or why you fail during the process.

'You do not understand your fear thermometer, how to control your thoughts from historical programming or how to break free of those blueprints.'

There is the probability at this point of it recurring, sometimes repeatedly, for damaging thought patterns take root and create automatic, repetitive programmes deep in the subconscious mind. On experiencing any perceived failure, this mindset will take you out of trying again for a better result.

'You are now continually generating cycles of dissatisfaction from operating on autopilot, and its managing ninety-five per cent of your behaviours.'

This behaviour is responsible for assuring you it was a mistake to try and you refute the process. A completely altered habit pattern is now required to take you beyond your current state and into a changed reality.

'Patterns of thought get re-enforced through repetition of tasks; your brain will obey the programming you continuously impress upon it.'

Wasting too much time on things that bring unhappiness and fret, establish new thought waves and in turn, new beliefs by this very act. Donald Hebb, a Canadian neuropsychologist, who was known for his work in the field of associative learning. Discovered the theory that: *'Neurons that wire together, fire together.'* Additional studies expanding on this principle, scientifically prove how the brain develops when infused with fresh knowledge, concluding that:

'Continuing to think a repeated thought with feeling causes neurons to start firing in the brain. When sustained over several weeks, you strengthen those thought connections. Now you are building a structure to form a brand-new programme inside your brain. A cluster of neuro-synapses continues to form, and a new file and habit created.'

This form's the brain's ability to associate and recall. Networks of neurons are being formed continuously, depending on the information you are feeding your mind.

'The quality of what you learn can empower or disempower you. This is the law, and it's always working with perfect exactitude. If you use this process regarding a negative outcome, you will bring about the very thing you are trying to avoid, as your brain is only following your requests and a pre-programmed set of beliefs that are familiar to it.

Now you have contributed to a formula unconsciously, to direct your senses outward to the external world, to reaffirm that which you impress onto your subconscious. Understanding develops with emotional experiences, learned behaviour, or input from others. Examples are walking, riding a bike, playing a sport, operating a computer, or driving a car. You can also learn very restrictive things too depending on what you have been exposed to during childhood and early youth. (*This is the imprinting period for all human beings*). If the impact has been negative, it often manifests as anger, low self-worth, low confidence, abuse, addiction, or violence once the individual becomes an adult. These beliefs require exposure to a particular environment coupled with repetitive actions over long periods. This causes a person to become so programmed by their surroundings; they behave a certain way. The exact same process happens when learning a new skill; you reach a proficiency level by the number of times you perform it creating a new file; it is now automatic.

'You can alter thought states; you can change paradigms and become a far better version of yourself than the one you are perceiving. It begins with awareness of anything you want to alter or change.'

You can begin to restructure the very matter in your head using neuroscience. The problem was never something peripheral but the unconscious effects of a conditioned brain. Many people think you need strong willpower to make a lasting change; it has nothing to do with this process, for it requires new associations to anything you wish to achieve or habits you need to break.

'You have chemically and neurologically become addicted to the feelings you attach your attention and energy to daily. Therefore, it can be tough to break those unhealthy patterns.'

You can only engage willpower for so long before old thoughts and beliefs resurface and override the process causing you to forego the mission in favour of a more comfortable choice. One of the best ways to reprogram your mind is by reading or listening to new things every day. Having the capacity to move beyond everything you deem familiar is at the forefront of change. Learning is not enough; it is also vital to implement the material whenever you can for new thought patterns to begin to take shape.

'When this principle is employed, and you do it often enough, you create new pathways in your brain. The benefit of combining this with massive repetitive action opens the door for an entirely new internal dialogue. This is the secret formula to take you beyond your usual behaviours and onto the other side.'

Stop choosing continuous holding patterns, instead learn to resist the negative self-talk and thoughts, by increasing your awareness of them, or you will keep returning to your old programmes that encourage a victim mindset.

'With any habitual thought, you need to interrupt the sequence, do the work required to raise your value and deservedness bar. When you do not feel enough, you will unconsciously obstruct and resist the changes necessary for transformation. Lack of self-love always leads to self-sabotaging actions and will prevent what you want from getting through to you.'

Everyone has these limitations to some degree, gaining the knowledge from positive resources like this book, along with the material available from the internet, can create a brand-new roadmap for you to follow. Start by forgiving yourself from anything that haunts or hampers you, open your closet (*your mind*) and begin the process of liberation from the skeletons that live there. I urge you to give yourself emotional permission to let go of these bonds for they cause only obstruction. Work on building new firm structures within your mind and when an opportunity presents itself, those old blocks that made you doubt, or trigger your risk thermometer to activate, can fall away. Those battles stem from your subconscious mind triggered from a past program, *'your script',* the one you got taught and all it knows at this time is it needs to protect you and keep you safe.

'Your thoughts will explore your memory banks to find supporting reasons as to why you shouldn't move beyond your comfort zone.'

It is the same with any goal or dream you are trying to attain. Your fears and disappointments are generated by what your mind is repeatedly playing—the excuses, the denial, the self-hate, those conversations you relentlessly have in your head. Over and over, around, and around you go, never escaping and searching endlessly to protect your honour when it all falls flat. This is what human's do, you chastise yourselves incessantly and go right back to the harmful programme that kept you in the unhappy camp way too long, preventing any progress.

You will find the things you are trying to escape from, will keep on showing up until you learn the workings of your mind and how to alter it by changing thoughts. The mechanics of your brain are universal; every single person who invests in self-education can develop the skill to change their stories and, ultimately, their life.

'You each have a reticular activating system (RAS), and this is a network of neurons in the brain stem. Its purpose is to ultimately facilitate your behaviour and acts as the gatekeeper of information between your external sensory systems and the conscious mind. Some refer to it as the human filtration system.'

An Italian neurophysiologist discovered it at the University of Pisa in Italy. The results were published in 1949 in the Inaugural Volume of the Scientific Journal. He was one of three scientists at the time who linked wakefulness to a sequence of brain structures known as the reticular activating system. It is a small section of your brain near the top of the spinal column and has a diameter marginally larger than a pencil.

This is responsible for sifting through information continuously transferred through your five senses (*except smell which goes to your emotional centre*).

'No human can process the immense amounts of data thrown at it daily; your RAS chooses the most significant for your conscious mind to pay consideration to. It only allows what supports programmed thought patterns and disregards everything else, based on your beliefs.'

Let me explain? If you have mostly negative thoughts and actions, always living in expectation of the worst, your RAS can only mirror these thoughts and behaviours back through to you in the present moment. It will keep sending material to sustain those negative expectations, as it has never learned to look for anything else. Therefore, you will keep having upsetting and restrictive encounters. It can never stop; your whole life will be a repeat performance of this until your thoughts change. Learning and applying one new thing daily to modify your usual pattern, will start the internal process required for new thought waves to fire and wire. It takes time to form this fresh structure as your old paradigms have been there for years. The good news, though is after thirty to ninety days of any new repetitive action, you begin forming a whole new set of connections within your brain, so stick with it.

'Repeated thoughts over a period, cause conscious thinking waves to fire and wire, imprinting the sub-conscious mind with new beliefs, this creates a brand-new story on which you can build from.'

This process is evident in people who are optimistic and cheerful most of the time, too, they are merely batting from a different angle. People think they are lucky and good things follow them around like magic tricks, this is not the case. They see the world with a vastly different perspective, and their expectations are the opposite of the previous person. This programs their RAS to see opportunities instead of obstacles and allows the right stuff to pass through their filtration system, ensuring the '*magic*' will keep on showing up for them. When I learnt this process all those years ago, to unlock the code; I knew I had to share it. You must be willing and eager to look at a substitute, one you haven't already tried, learn about your mind and how it ticks, understand exactly how it keeps you stuck in repetitive patterns. Through their release, you become destined to meet your new objectives.'

'It's time to open the door of chance and carve your new path. To step into this altered reality, you must fully employ self-empowering thoughts, self-belief, and the deservedness required to create those optimal outcomes.'

Depending on your upbringing, whether you are fearful and worried or excited and hopeful, your brain can only function from two podia. One is to protect you, and the other is for you to thrive, that is it! So, unfortunately, due to the number of negative influences evident in society, an innumerable amount of people chose to live in protective cocoons a lot of the time, you will recognise it as the comfort zone, your place of perceived certainty and safety. Collective consciousness is similar to the herding mentality, where large percentages of the population become hypnotised or driven to conform through messages in culture, television, and media feeds. You question very little but complain a lot, without realising you are contributing to this very movement, one inherently biased towards controlling your thoughts.

'If you cannot think independently, without needing to alter your values to align with what you are watching, seeing, or hearing, you will be powerless to disengage from it.'

Only your uneasiness of appearing different, or an inability to question those opinions prevent you from exercising an alternative thought.

'You are always programming your personal computer (your subconscious mind) with your input and its always listening.'

Here is where your power lies and the chance to pursue better, get ready to experience a whole new scope of possibility and expect a completely different destination. I learnt this from a personal experience and quickly realised when pushed onto that track, just how much I was missing. When you see it, you will never be likely to question your findings ever again, for it reveals a whole new realm of chance. I don't want you to wait or get to rock bottom before you transform. I want you to take the reins now, set those wheels in motion and learn all you can on this subject.

'You are without a doubt wired to find a purpose for being in this place, at your very core lies a desire you were born with, a relentless quest for significance and a deeper meaning to life.'

Your subconscious is always in charge; when something unfamiliar appears, your reaction to it will register where you are on this expedition. Those jolts are the indicators encouraging you to have a swing in perception towards a more unconventional route. Regrettably, when you do not heed its messages, you can remain shackled to dead-end jobs or unhealthy relationships often for years, leaving you frustrated and disillusioned. If you have a painful past attached to emotions that keep you in a victim state, it is down to your inability to live in the present moment, causing you to remain a prisoner to your past and those contaminated thoughts. *YOU* are holding yourself back by refusing to see an alternative; you must take a chance and contemplate these ideas for only a fool would reject them now without researching their merit.

'According to scientific research, the Conscious Mind contributes less than 10 per cent of total brain function. That means the subconscious represents around 90 per cent. The more significant part of thinking happens in the subconscious, the captain controlling most of your behaviours.'

If you do not learn to reprogramme and gain mastery over the beliefs that reside there, you will be unable to make better choices. Fear halts progress and can impair the formation of long-term memories and damage certain parts of the brain. Your hippocampus consolidates data from short-term to long-term memory. When this process is interrupted, it becomes challenging for an individual to regulate that fear leading to persistent feelings of anxiety. This can be a causative factor responsible for creating undue stress to the recipient. When a person endures his state for too long, It can affect their physical and mental health.

'Everyone is afraid of something, and you learn to think this way from an event or experience in your past. You feel the emotion of fear in your amygdala, the front portion of the temporal lobe. This part of your brain alerts you to these feelings, and it also provides the awareness required for you to identify them in others.

When you are in this heightened state, it transfers through changes you will feel physically in your body. This flight or fight response causes adrenaline to be released into your system and at the same time, reduces blood flow to the frontal lobe responsible for logical thinking. Now the parts of your brain accountable for survival take over. You will recognise it outwardly as a change in body language. This can manifest as a person defending themselves or choosing to withdraw from an action that fuels their disagreement. It can also produce an aggressive tone due to a perceived threat.

Regardless of how it is displayed outwardly, at that moment, what they feel is real for them. When fear becomes crippling, you cannot gain control or perspective, it crushes dreams, ends relationships, destroys opportunities, and kills visions for better, this is due to uncertainty and can affect your life in terribly negative ways. There is a process to supersede fear through confidence as awareness is needed to facilitate a belief towards something more optimistic, even if you can't see it in the present.

'Being closed to potential causes you to stay in a constant state of protection, and this encourages a hard-wired response into yourself, your fear will kick into action, and come up with

every excuse in the book, giving you permission to take yourself right out of the game.'

You can break through the impasse, though it will take time and patience. You must develop the propensity to silence your thoughts and any from others who promote this mindset. Those influencers who perpetrate these acts do so by using the transference and persuasion of their own limitations. They intend for you to follow their lead and disengage from the climb.

'These individuals are also operating from conditioned responses just like you, so do not judge them, they haven't found their path yet, so they do not have the privilege of destroying yours.'

It is crucial to focus only on yourself; it's not your job to fix anyone, so direct your efforts towards working on your worthiness instead and lead by example to effect change.

'Everyone has limitations to differing degrees; it's unavoidable when you live from past programmes.'

You must 'Feel the fear and do it anyway'. Do not postpone actions that raise fear in you or convince yourself its best to wait until you have additional assistance to conquered it.

Understand to defeat those emotions you must start to operate the other way round. By charging head-on into the quest, you overcome your doubts; it is always through the doing that you let it fall away. Only face forward now as you cannot reverse time, continuing to do the same things in light of what you now know will drive you right back into a victim state. I encourage you to learn meditation and find one that resonates with you the best; it will teach you to take yourself out of your head and train your mind to be at peace without the constant chatter that relentlessly revolves around in there.

'Scientific discoveries prove the grey matter in your head can be moulded by continuous learning. Once new pathways are formed, accepted as true and adopted into a new routine, you begin a process that alters behaviours, reactions, and values.'

When physically or emotionally tense, your adrenal glands send catecholamines into your blood in the form of norepinephrine and epinephrine. *(your stress hormones).* Meditation counteracts this by increasing the activity of the parasympathetic nervous system, causing the adrenal medulla to decrease the production of them. Simultaneously, this process boosts serotonin and dopamine *(your feel-good hormones),* creating feelings of peace and calm. I use Dr Joe Dispensa's meditation from his progressive workshop I attended in 2019. Within a couple of weeks of consistently following the process, I was astonished and grateful for the level of calm I felt and the opportunities that kept showing up. When your mind is clear, and no longer consumed by doubt or lack; you allow the door of the universe to open for all manner of wonder to rush in.

'During the practice of meditation, you can completely disconnect from the busyness of life and recharge. Add in visualisation with emotion, and you become enveloped by good feelings without restrictions and a fuller connection to your imagination. Here you birth a better version of yourself in a future state, doing it continually sends powerful signals to the subconscious telling it you want this picture instead. I will go into this topic a little deeper later in this chapter.'

When you are in a stressed state, you live in fight or flight, focusing on survival. Running on adrenalin rapidly depletes energy reserves, and your concentration will be severely affected. If this is endured for extensive periods, your body creates an environment to cause internal systems to get knocked out of balance. You are now downregulating your genes, which seriously impairs immune function and has a detrimental effect on a system that works 24/7 to keep you well and in an atmosphere of equilibrium.

'The evolution of nature and humans shows a system created to encourage cooperation and not competition. Yet in the current timeline, there is more rivalry and separation than ever. This is in direct conflict with your source and does not nurture an internal harmonious environment. There is an invisible bond of interconnectedness between life on this planet. Those who cultivate a supportive mindset, understand the fusion of that connection and how important it must become for everyone to benefit.'

An ecological unit endorsing feelings of security and abundance is key to your contentment. You become aware you live within a frame centred around duality, which shows you the difference between those contrasts.

Yin and yang, black and white, good and bad, right and wrong etc. Learn to adapt to a universe in constant motion, and your mental and physical wellbeing won't feel so challenged by stresses or burdens placed upon it. Your bodies designed to heal itself from the discord within it, the viruses and bacteria that attack it every day, broken bones fix, cuts repair, depression, and anxiety lifts.

'Your brain is more powerful than any supercomputer, and its job is to work in harmony with your body's natural defences to do whatever it takes to preserve your life, especially when under attack from any foreign enemy.'

A great example of this authority is the brain's ability to adapt when a person suffers a stroke. It recognises a particular part has sustained an injury. Depending on the extent of the impairment; it can begin to re-route around the area and join up new electrical networks called cortical remapping. This occurs as a functional response to the damage, and it is how many people who suffer these severe obstructions, can retrain the mind through continuous thought actions. Working with professionals specialising in repetitive physical exercises can restore the many activities capable before the accident. If your brain can do something as awesome as this, how much do you think it can support you when it comes to reprogramming disempowering beliefs?

'You are accountable for your life of unhappiness and negativity, you have allowed in the perfect conditions, responsible for damage to your physical and mental form.'

Extensive mental exposure to this field automatically transfers onto your physical body, and this is where you will feel the pain. All things begin inside the mind, and you are controlling that machine.

'The power of the grey matter that resides between your ears is a phenomenal piece of kit, one you give surprisingly little notice to most of the time. Every day your brains are making decisions based on choices, some are made in seconds by your subconscious mind, without you having any awareness of them.'

Those thoughts are a mental process letting you see the world through your lens and coding. These beliefs dwell in the subconscious mind and are programmed during the imprinting periods in childhood and early youth. The most significant percentage of your thoughts are unconscious and driven by a pre-programmed roadmap that has been in there for years. Your habitual patterns are the ones you must alter as this is where the barriers lie. Those paradigms are the basis of what has moulded you into who you are. When you appreciate your views, principles, and values get reinforced by what you see every day in the natural world, you can begin the work required to change it. This can set you free from envy, discord, judgement, and so many illnesses associated with stress.

'The mass between your ears, inside your skull, drives understanding on the world outside. Yet the irony is your brain has never seen the light of day, so it creates the visual representations required through your five senses, to give you a graphic interpretation of how you view the world.'

To become the master of your mind, you must learn to monitor damaging thoughts, by instantly changing course as soon as you become aware of them or are alerted to a recurring pattern. Most of the time, you are thinking the same things, regardless of the day of the week you are on. This is your hard-wired design keeping you within the familiar, so you feel safe in the space you inhabit. Become a creator of new thought, which offers an opportunity to see what life could look like when you inject it with an uncommon replacement.

'How do you come to understand what the power of thinking is, and how it has the potential to adjust your life when you learn, understand and apply how to alter it?'

Any action you initiate and any decision you make had its origin in thought first. You connect that thought to an activity that ends with an emotional response (***how you feel***). The thoughts you think repeatedly are the most important ones, as they are responsible for influencing the behaviour you will emit.

To transform the core dialogue of an individual, there must be a commitment to do something different every day, to replace the old story that has been continually playing.

'Everything is energy in this universe; it is all around you, in all things, including you. When you have a collection of these energy particles, it becomes matter, so although what you see feels solid, at a subatomic level everything is vibrating at a different frequency, as this world is a continuously moving field.'

How does this relate to thoughts? If everything you are and everything you do, is energetic, then your thoughts carry that frequency too. The manifestation you bring to your sphere of experience, are drawn by your ability to align with a frequency you desire to have. Your thoughts are the start of the process to generates those outcomes.

'Most people pull in what they are trying to avoid, as their thoughts and actions are predominately negative, and the world you live in can only return what you give out.'

Negative equals negative, drama, worry, depression, and anxiety caused by experiences outside of you and kept alive in your mind through those thoughts and actions daily.

'You get onto a revolving door with no idea how to get off or change direction. You won't be able to if nothing changes in you and that starts between your ears.'

Scientists from the National Research Nuclear University have studies using a laser device to record thoughts in humans called infrasonic waves. These low-frequency vibrations are formed by physiological processes, of the heart beating, along with blood flow and respiratory actions and have a bearing on emotional stress. These findings show thoughts are driven by feelings and can significantly affect how you function, dependent on what is happening in your life. Knowing this information, do you think it's possible to become a person who can change the direction of thought to create improvement?

'Yes, absolutely. Now how can this be done?'

Gratitude is seriously underrated as a vehicle for raising the vibration of an individual. Yet, it is the one thing to cultivate appreciation and remove competition when practised regularly and with emotional attachment.

Gratitude fires and wires a whole new set of connections that form new patterns of thought. You cannot be down, unhappy, or angry and grateful simultaneously; it's physically impossible.

'So, driving your attention towards what you believe is missing, prevents you from exercising the thoughts required to give you what you genuinely want. Choosing new habits towards the evolution of your current state brings about better life experiences.'

Your past programming originates from your childhood; as your mind must stay within those limits to feel safe; it's just what you were taught to become familiar with. You cannot change memories; still, you can change your association with them, which holds the key to your freedom. At the front of the brain lies the prefrontal cortex; the part responsible for elevated intellectual function, it is involved in planning and promotes personality development.

'When trying to build new behaviours, you engage the functions of the prefrontal cortex; you're thinking brain. You will have to repeat whatever thought or task you are intent on altering and do it enough times, for the new programme to automatically become wired and strengthened within your mind to make it normal for you.'

It has been long known the basal ganglia a group of structures found deep within the cerebral hemispheres of the brain, interacts closely with the prefrontal cortex.

The basal ganglia detect the right conditions to perform motor functions and facilitate the frontal cortex in executing such actions at the appropriate time. It can recall triggers that produce replicated habits to support the brain's reward system. Some evidence indicates it chooses behaviours you will have found gratifying previously and is a causative factor in the forming of habits.

Therefore, repetitive actions are necessary to change the pre-programmed incentives; When those changes make you more content and happier, it prevents you from slipping back into limiting cycles. Over time those new repetitive thought actions are automatically uploaded to your subconscious. When they become part of your operating programme, you will routinely start to default to this new replacement, until it becomes your new normal.

'So, the more you perform anything new, and you do it often enough you are rewiring the internal system of yourself and this amazing phenomenon is called neuroplasticity.'

The act of duplication to gain a result will take you beyond normal and into exploratory ground. With ample conviction, commitment, self-belief, and discipline, you can rewrite your script and move beyond what you deem comfortable. The practice of meditation and mindfulness can assist you with this method by altering your mind state. Meditation gives you time for contemplation and the capacity to take you past the analytical mind and into relaxed brainwave states, in this space the conscious mind closes off and the subconscious mind awakens, here is where your historical beliefs, habitual patterns and paradigms reside.

'The electromagnetic fluctuations quiet the nervous system, permitting your brain to shift into a significantly lower vibration, you enter a dream-like state, and the body becomes unaware of its physical form. These states of consciousness create a magnetic force and produce effects on your whole body when practised regularly. There is a tremendous amount of electrical activity being produced inside your brain when you are in this meditative state, and you become open to suggestion. This starts the process of literally altering your mind. Neurons start communication with each other through

synchronized electrical pulses, producing increased learning and creativity.'

This practice takes time to reach a proficiency level, and your body and mind will fight you and urge you to move, by filling your thoughts with other jobs you think you should be doing. Your mind does not like to do anything that is not already a part of your programme. It is vital to stay with it, though, until you surrender your will and master the process. Once you have developed the ability to focus on your breathing and the space around you, add visualisation (***mental pictures of what you wish your new reality to look like***). Inject it with the emotion you will feel when you have it, and you create an extraordinary combination to produce outstanding results.

Note: you can find a large variety of free guided meditations on Youtube to get started, please remember always to use headphones and conduct your meditations in a quiet place where you will not be interrupted.

'Using this process daily stirs an awareness within, you become calmer, more focused, and appreciate the joy in the simplest of things. You will stop striving as everything you need is already within you. Realigning to this universal field

opens doors that were always there but due to your blueprint you were unable to see them.'

Making this a regular part of your schedule generates the most amazing synchronicities to happen, this has been my experience, and from my research, the same has happened to many others. Meditation moves brain waves from a higher to a lower frequency that changes how you feel on a deep internal level.

'If you are on the fence with this one, at least try the process for thirty days before you throw in the towel. Though ultimately, for the best results, it must become a part of your daily routine from now on.'

The benefits of meditation are explained through the habitual process of training your mind to focus and redirect your thoughts. You can use it to increase awareness of yourself and your surroundings. Here is a list of excellent benefits you can expect from meditating every day, it almost makes it a no-brainer, if I can persuade you something as simple as this, could make such a difference to your life then why wouldn't you?

- *Lowers Anxiety and Depression*
  - *Decreases Stress*
  - *Enhances Concentration*
- *Boosts the Immune System and helps Manage Pain.*
  - *Promotes Emotional-Wellbeing.*
  - *Heightens Self-Awareness*
  - *Extends Attention Span*
  - *Improves Sleep*

Alternatively, there is a growing interest in Mindfulness too, with classes and online workshops for those with interest in finding out more. This method demonstrates how to become more attentive to your feelings in the now. You achieve this psychological process by intentionally bringing your awareness to experiences taking place in the present moment without judgement. It identifies feelings that may be negative and teach you how to differentiate those sensations when ignited. In turn, this helps to release the hold they have on you, replacing it with insight, now you can let them pass through without any need to react.

'Although mindfulness might not reduce the thoughts that are troubling you, it can help you rationalise your perspective on

it. Adopting this strategy addresses it quickly so you can get on with your life. You produce a healthier platform with altered states of being and reap the benefits of living in the present where your power dwells.'

When you spend your time channelling your attention in the wrong way, it produces the most formidable force—this energy controls thoughts, actions, emotions and finally your outcomes.

'You have a brain that is malleable and can be changed and modified to reflect a better experience so develop it, and use it to create your biggest supporter, instead of your main opponent.'

These chapters explain the workings of your mind, and with it, how you operate as a human being. Learn and apply it to your life. Then you can identify undesirable behaviours and comprehend the barriers you build by initiating the means to replace them.

*Stop holding yourself back
and start climbing now!!!!*

Geraldine Mair

- CHAPTER FIVE -

PULLING IT ALL

TOGETHER

QUOTE

'I want to stand for awareness of opportunity, what can be attained with the right mental attitude and conscious responsiveness, that there is indeed an unlimited power in making a choice.

You need to get to a place beyond the pain, one where you are no longer willing to tolerate any injustice for your life and just decide what you are going to become, then set about making that happen with massive action.'

Geraldine Mair

Your inner critic will continue to keep you stuck in places you should be capable of moving away from. It's the despondent voice continuing to rise whenever you confront it with anything new or a change in direction. This is responsible for the emotional paralysis you will feel and stop any evolution or advancement into other areas. Stop this noise, it's incredibly harmful, and it will continue to reinforce your feelings of lack, lack of confidence, lack of self-worth and lack of ability.

'You have over 60,000 thoughts in a day; unfortunately, 95% of them are the same as yesterday, so, you will keep producing the same outcomes. To change, it becomes imperative to keep doing things unfamiliar to you as often as you can, this swings the percentage more in your favour.'

When you pull away from chances due to fear, you are unconsciously burying a considerable part of yourself, and the possibilities waiting for you. Your central opponent is in no way beneficial to your wellbeing, the only thing it can ever help you with is over-analysis of situations.

This is neither healthy nor helpful and is responsible for anxiety, and a weight of guilt that will continually pull you down.

'The fear you are feeling is a typical one, it shows up when you feel threatened by change and is your inner adversary encouraging you to stay exactly where you are. Life is short, so push aside that opponent and go for it.'

Build your awareness of the barricades you continue to construct, particularly ones preventing you from harnessing your power over any situation or finding an answer to resolve it. The solutions and actions will come when you understand the operating system within your mind is responsible. Identify your worries, triggers, loves, and dislikes, so you can use that information to adjust your opinions. You must not adapt only a little and then settle into a new norm as a mechanism to cope; that is where you are now. Instead, get ready to completely re-write your programme as an opportunity to start building a winner's resilience.

Remember what you wanted when you were young, and you didn't have the impediments that hold you back now. Reconnect to your imagination and lead the charge for new thinking, as this will inspire change.

'Young children will openly tell you when you ask them what they want to be when they grow up, producing all manner of

wonderful things; there are no obstacles at this point for in their mind they can be, do or have anything in this life.'

They dream of the perfect pictures they see on TV or in the Disney films, believing real life can be just like that. They model their visions on what they see from favourite football players to pop singers.

'Do you remember a time when you felt just like that?'

It only became evident to me on speaking with clients years later, many of those dreams had been rejected, and replaced by an expectation of someone else's standards. A well-meaning parent who steered you down a road you wouldn't have picked on your own. A teacher who stated you didn't have the skills required to become what you envisioned, or a boss who was constantly on your case and left you feeling as if you were unworthy of your post or disempowered every day.

'You have become a casualty like so many, trapped in a system of allowing others to dictate your ability and competence, seriously hindering your capacity to rise.'

This mindset is constructed over the years and steals those clear visions prevalent in your youth. It shuts down the resourcefulness and imagination of your malleable minds. On reaching adulthood, you grow the negative stimuli to generate doubts, leaving you questioning your worth, aptitude or deservedness. Those foundations are firmly formed, and conformity born, thus establishing a structural society you need to fit into.

'When enough time passes, the dominate thought patterns of the now young adults, are conditioned to accept those external inputs.'

Their dreams replaced by the belief it was no more than an overactive immature mind. Once you buy into that idea, your aspirations and desires fall into the realms of impossible fantasy, ones that were never attainable anyway.

'Do you remember the life you envisioned before you grew up and joined the attitude of the masses? You get in a pack like a herd of cattle and stay caught for years, fear becomes your default, and you settle into what is familiar, this is your danger zone.'

It will become more difficult to cut those cords the longer you have lived with them, choosing to surround yourself with people and experiences that mirror those beliefs, will support an embedded structure, and keep you in the same place. It's hard to let go of this because you attach to your tribe and the strong values that live within that group are fierce. Your requirement to belong supersedes everything else and thwarts openness towards other truths.

'You will continually search for evidence to support the road you now find yourself on; as you need this to make sense of your life, as humans, you must find meaning for your choices.'

Maybe now you can understand why you do what you do, I can instil a theory to help you with those inner conflicts. Spending time with people who have managed to transcend their limitations, proves it can be done and helps you keep going.

'Accepting a collective intention either from another person or through various media channels grows destructive beliefs and contributes to activities that promote separation and industrial slaves.'

When your mind is in chaos, your IQ goes down, buying into this kind of relentless toxicity makes it exceedingly difficult to find a way past it. You are connecting those thought waves I spoke about in chapter four, the ones responsible for building a whole new set of beliefs that never positively serve you. You must see gratitude for your life, what you have no matter how large or small you perceive it to be and nurture this emotion daily. This will give you enough resilience to counteract the pessimism, especially if better is to find its way through to you.

'Expressing gratitude, raises your vibration, connecting you to the universal field, when you are in a better place mentally, it alerts you to the next opportunity when it hits, for you will become expectant and attuned to noticing it.'

Sticking your heels in and refusing to change can only guarantee the life you have will persist, the one you say you don't want, and it can manifest in so many ways. You may suffer depression or feel overwhelmed with life or the emotions and events that brought you to this place. You could be someone who's attention is always on what others have achieved, and you feel envious and resentful, or you could be working every hour God sends to try to make ends meet due to a pre-set expectation to be the best, and it's now hurting your head and your heart.

'You don't know what you don't know, and thinking you do not need to grow is only your ego talking. The requirement for fresh learning is a prerequisite for growth, mental and physical; it should never stop regardless of age.'

Take hope from what you have learned; it doesn't have to be this way; you can make a choice and a commitment to do something for yourself. Don't settle; it is not integral to your source. The Trifecta of Awareness begins in your *mind*; in unison with your *gut* instinct and transcends through your *heart*. When these three factors are in harmony, it boosts the potential of every human machine. It's time to evolve as technology has and offer yourself those choices; you deserve to know the critical components of your mind and body, and how it works. The difference this can make will be life-altering.

'You can support yourself and your family by teaching them how to be mindful of what they let into their headspace, increasing kindness and love as the guiding force, instead of fear, resentment, and shame. Reducing those external stressors causes the imagination to flourish, replacing it with a vision full of possibility.'

Once you learn this, please pay it forward by conveying that knowledge to your family and friends. It takes only one to make a difference, for when the message is powerful enough, and the behaviour is evident, it won't take long for others to see the value it has given to your life and make the jump themselves.

'Refuse to go in the same direction as everyone else, accepting the same things. It doesn't make it right; look around you; it's preserving old habits and producing lives that are miserable. It's like going backwards and expecting the universe to redirect your course without your participation.'

Learned behaviour is adopted and handed down through the generations. Those beliefs and limitations get taught by those who surrounded you, much of it unconscious and without malice. This happens because there is no understanding of the automatic programming it creates, blocking uncapped potential. When you choose to spend time researching this material, it builds a better account of your past and the behaviours associated with it. Apply this knowledge to shorten the time you have to tolerate uncomfortable situations and give yourself the gift of insight.

'When you are prepared to do better, you become equipped to choose better. Improved choices always lead to a better life.'

Social media systems like YouTube and Audible, have an abundance of information to assist you on your quest for knowledge. Change becomes possible when you remove the ceiling on habitual patterns, ones that have stopped you from receiving what was always warranted. Realise the actions you choose to take part in daily are responsible for forming neurochemical, molecular changes within your cells. The scientific name given to these are better known as neurons, and this is the vehicle within the human brain transmitting electrical signals like messengers.

'As a human being, you are an extraordinarily complex system, your subconscious mind effortlessly carries out your bodies requirements for life, without you having any awareness of it.'

Your breathing, your heart continually beating, your hormones and the job they do daily to try to keep your body in balance, the usual patterns that you follow as soon as you rise. Showering, cleaning your teeth, getting dressed etc. These actions work on autopilot, with little thought, they are programmed into the subconscious mind years before and have become a habit.

'Your mind controls the information you absorb every moment, filtering and storing anything of interest based on your beliefs and values, and discards surplus material you deem unnecessary to your requirements.'

You are equipped to alter states of thought through a process called neuroplasticity. This procedure causes networks to strengthen or weaken over time, depending on the information being absorbed or lack of it. Now you can appreciate your brain's ability to fortify or erode those connections, as explained in chapter four. This is the vehicle for your mental strength to change during your life span. You can build new, more empowering synaptic connections within grey matter, ones that become better go-to auto programmes to alter your behaviours through repetitive actions of any new learnings. Anything you choose to adopt as your brand-new truth can become familiar when enough time gets invested in the process. The authority is in you, and you are the only one who can change direction. No one is coming to rescue you from your despair; you must keep on stretching your capacity and education if you are to conquer those thoughts, the ones that restrict any effort upwards.

'Let this become the moment you grip the joy of your life and silence the voice that questions your worth. Commit to releasing anything with fear or dread attached to it, for only in thought do you keep these notions alive. They are not your destiny or your identity unless you choose to make it so.'

Try to stop using labels as a means of identification as this is so restrictive and only hinders you. Your past is not you; your illness is not you; your broken relationship is not you; your difficult upbringing or lack of education is not you. These are evidence of a past you accepted as accurate at the time. I hope you can see the rational in it now, and release the baggage preventing you from celebrating your true worth. Find your way back to self-love if you wish to create bonds and connections with others; for without this vital step, it will be tough to give to anyone else effectively. Once you realise this fundamental fact, you can begin to retrain your thoughts through learning new things. You may have to take down old demons and forgive yourself or others to feel that self-love, but through this development, it will lead you towards a more illuminated life. You become what you believe.

'These internal lies marinate over decades, millions of bites of information and the culmination of days you have notched up until now. Add in the people who have been influencing you, and you have multiple areas you can improve on.'

Once again, bring your awareness to this present moment, knowing what you know now, do you still believe you have limits? You don't, you are infinite, so if life is not giving you what you need, want, or deserve, then change your tribe, your career, your partner, or your environment when it feels wrong it usually is, and you cannot imagine how it affects your human psyche. Let me share a story with you to clarify how surroundings matter and the importance of choosing the right team for the best results. When you actively choose a positive and nurturing community, it is scientifically proven to lower illness records relating to stress and heart disease.

This phenomenon is better known as the "Roseto Effect".

An independent study conducted in the 1960s examined a population of Italian immigrants in the town of Roseto in the United States. The findings are published in the Journal of the American Medical Association.

'The findings stipulated that no one under 47 years of age died from a heart attack, the rate of heart attacks in men over 65 was half the national average, and the death rates from all causes were 35% lower than anywhere else.'

After analysing the data, the scientists confirmed diet was not a factor, as they did not have the money for good nutrition. They worked in slate and quarry mines in harsh environments, fraught with risks due to lack of health and safety. They frequently ate meat deep-fried in lard, and many smoked and drank alcohol. This would typically produce appalling health statistics and yet, the researchers observed whilst living in the town, the key variation was a significant, cohesive, and equally encouraging, close-knit community structure, with stable family and neighbourhood ties. The elderly were not forgotten but admired and respected; this, in turn, built a robust unshakable bond, concluding the power to form strong relationships with others, directly affected heart disease risk.

'This ground-breaking research proves connection and a feeling of being needed and loved, are vital to the immune system in all humans.'

What could this world look like if you took steps to implement the same values evident in 'Roseta'. Imagine communities that actively looked after each other. Places of work could become hives of industrial energy, like bees working together towards a common goal, instead of treading over each other on the way to the top. Family time would be appreciated instead of competing with other things believed to have more merit.

'I have witnessed important things being placed on the back burner to get ahead, pushed aside to gain more, get more or be the best, wanting what others have and sacrificing everything to get it. It creates nothing but a disproportionate amount of unnecessary pressure, while missing out on the gifts that are right under your nose.'

Science has already joined the dots to provide enough evidence between stress and body systems. When you generate an environment that places those structures into decline, you knock your body out of homeostasis (*body, mind, balance*). When you do it for an extended period, it downgrades genes responsible in the body for keeping your immune system healthy; this has a knock-on effect creating risks that actively protects you from infection. Considerable investments are pumped into research for cures to multiple disorders. Yet "why" as a nation, is there no consideration towards replacing disease management for a wellness culture instead.

It's time to take responsibility for your, mental, spiritual, and physical health; you must surround yourself with people and a culture that encourages unity and support. Think about your daily routine, the environments you live in, where you go to work or interact with others, is it causing you stress? Do you feel excited and fulfilled being there? Or do you feel drained and dreaming of an escape route one that offers you a brighter horizon.

'This is your time, your opportunity to grab that chance.
Think about the contribution you are making to the whole and
how your actions and decisions affect it; you will see the

benefit of a healthy choice when your goal is towards service. I believe this is the answer if your objective is to make a difference.'

Everyone has a duty to impact the planet positively. Let it begin by sowing seeds, ones that grow something better for yourself, the environment, your circumstances, and those who you place your trust in daily.

'Knowledge and the application of it is where positive power lies.'

Discovering the sources of your stress and how it impacts your life can help you gain control. Applying strategies to diffuse it can help you improve connections and with it the opportunity to live in a more nurturing environment. The study proves it lowers disease and offers a more contented life like 'Roseta, so, perhaps it's time to alter how you act or who you keep company with, more so if you are constantly sick or suffering from excessive stress. Make sure if you feel constrained, it's important to voice your opinion, especially when it directly involves you, your family or your quality of life.'

'When you actively choose to suspend your values to fit in to feel included, it will eventually affect your mental and physical health. You will feel the discord internally, circling

you like a shroud. If you continue to be someone else in conflict with your source, your path to joy will ultimately become an exceptionally long and cumbersome one.'

Get off this path now. It's time to comprehend those who do not value you. Holding you back elevates their wounded ego, yet the price you will ultimately pay will be your own ability to rise. Their fight must continue to guarantee significance within their groups; no one wants to be in a place where there is an elevated structure of importance depending on who you are. Real connection is always based on equality.

'Genuine friends encourage you, even if they are more or less successful than you, they never let you down, and always show up to cheer you on.'

Time to stop following and surrendering your morals for approval, sacrificing who you are for others will only keep you relevant for so long because eventually, it will erode who you authentically are—leaving you with nothing but regrets. Listen to your gut, alerting you to your choices and let go of social programming. Be bold enough to step away from the crowd as this will prevent anything from limiting you in this life. You are energy in motion, and you can tap into an endless ocean of strength on the inside, when you break this negative connection, what you will find just beyond this boundary, are the dreams and desires of your heart, and exactly how to get them. Refuse to entertain past hurts as this removes perpetual loops of disempowering actions and makes it much easier to get out from under the weight. The best way forward is to stop talking about your problems all the time to anyone that will listen, get your focus and attention onto more productive things and stop blaming others for how you feel. You have a choice, and it's a bad one when you continue to punish yourself for what you or another has done to you.

'No one and I mean no one can affect your mood unless you allow them to. When you take ownership of another person's actions, you become paralysed into believing they are responsible for how you feel.'

It is not uncommon for events to have an impact on your life, so you shouldn't beat yourself up about that, the real issues arise when you refuse to let it go and still hold on to it years or decades later. Do you want the rest of your life to look like this? Are you trapped in a destructive pattern, feeding these emotions, and living a fraction of your true self? Are you still convinced it's someone else's fault you can't create the life of your dreams?

Or are you whittling your days away in meaningless jobs and relationships that are fruitless because you believe this is it and there is no alternative? Now is the time to release those restrictions and step into your greatness.

'Look at my story; I came from a pre-programmed belief as many of you have, and it led to a job that paid poorly for a forty-hour week. I tolerated years of verbal abuse from managers above me because I believed they knew more than I did, were more intelligent than me, and my destiny was always to follow and never take any control. When I learned this information, I soon realised many things I had taken on board as an incorrect truth.'

With self-belief and sheer grit, I crawled out from under all of this and you can too. Take time to dissect your stories from the past; there will be many things within that narrative; you will find yourself questioning. No one should tolerate anything in this life that violates who they are as a human being. Living this way with so many untruths about yourself inevitably leads to a belief of a lesser worth. I've changed everything about my life, career, future, self-worth, confidence, endurance, and level of deservedness and trust me; I have had to let go of many things during that passage to find my purpose. I am no longer willing to entertain any negative energy and always stay calm regardless of who is delivering it.

'I refuse to give my power away to anyone intent on pushing my buttons or flicking my switch, it has taken time to get to this place and many trips and slips to hone that skill.'

I have never undertaken anything so worth it, though, and my inner strength always drives me now. I choose to disengage from drama and no longer give my time or energy to entertaining mindless nonsense. I live in the present moment because I can make a difference there, which is so liberating. Focusing on your temperament stops those outside influences from altering your state. Choose your mood always, and never give responsibility for it to anyone else. It is never what is said or done to you that causes the discord, but your reaction to it that fuels the endless cycle and keeps it relevant. Those who spend inordinate amounts of time grumbling life sucks yet do nothing to adjust that limbo, only have themselves to blame for their misery, for only through *MASSIVE ACTION* can any alternative be undertaken to revise that course.

'Excuses, denial, and blame are where unhappy souls live, those who never change the record, or their attitude can at no time expect anything better to show up. Conforming to outside

influences places additional burdens on an already stretched psyche, to give more, be more, produce more be happier etc.'

Releasing those blocks must become crucial for you, to appreciate you need to get so uncomfortable where you are that choosing a replacement becomes vital. Learned behavioural factors add credence to this load's weight and make specific groups more susceptible to following patterns directed by others. Your hurt can be very painful depending on the weight of the blow, or depth of the wound that caused it in the first place. This delivers an automatic, unconscious response from your brain, that continuously generates the same feelings produced by past triggers. Every time the sensation occurs, you feel overwhelmed again in your current timeline.

'Your necessity to hold onto it so tightly keeps it alive, when dealing with any mental stress; you must look deep inside to uncover the source that produced it.'

It's hard to let go of the things you feel give you your identity; I understand this very well, and it can cause real disputes within your mind. Your fear engages, and you move away from anything that makes you question it. Your past and the memories associated with that time are a way of recognising that identity, and what stands in front of you now? It builds a personality you have grown over many years of experience and recollections. If you are ready to adapt, you must take the key, open the door, and build a new character, one that frees you from that lifetime of inner torment.

'Are you ready to face your fear, and do it anyway?

Your sentiments are from long ago kept alive in the present. The happy moments you recall with fondness or the painful ones you often place far too much awareness on. At this juncture, it's critically important; you see the lessons weaved within them and give the least attention and energy to the ones that cause you anguish.

'Staying in any place when you are hurting, generates a perpetual unending, indeterminate state, and you turn out to be the very thing I expressed earlier in this chapter. A condition, an event, an illness, a bad relationship, a poor upbringing and the list goes on'.

I want the best life for you, one where you measure wealth through feelings of contentment, awareness of gratitude and appreciation of the beautiful things all around you. Always striving for more or wanting more is destructive, when will it ever be enough, when do you take your foot off the gas? And when do you stop feeling envious or jealous of others who have more?

Stop now, today, right at this moment!

There is no need to give any more to this, where has it got you up until this point? Think hard on this, when nothing is shifting in your experience, please do not waste any more time going through this sludge.

'YOU are creating the drama and bitterness, yes YOU! by your approach to it and your endless habitual actions that could be making you repel.'

As crazy as this seems many people stay in a place they associate with incredible pain, they choose to tolerate the situation, cave under the stress of it and end up at its mercy. They start to identify with their environment, and it becomes their personality. Because they have shouted about it for so long, they find it extremely hard to reverse from that position and start again.

'Living in a state of wretchedness and apathy because you believe your life needs to be one of personal punishment, is no way for anyone to live ever!'

Why not completely reinvent yourself, regardless of the consequences or what anyone else thinks? Let go of the baggage that gets carried around because of this mindset and decide you are worthy of love, love for yourself, love from others, joy, abundance, and peace. Happiness is your birthright, and it lives in the hearts of those longing for a space to express it. It really doesn't matter what has gone before or if you feel like a fraud, all that counts now is who you choose to become.

'The biggest challenge you will ever face in this life is to have the courage to say you've had enough and to mean it. It will only be when you reach this point; you can invite it in willingly and with an open heart. Now an opportunity to rise can emerge. This is your time, and this book is your sign that the change is long overdue.'

Understand you can be a person of significance and not one you have created from stories you told yourself for years about your past and the things you had to endure. Ruin is the road to transformation and salvation. The lowest points in life are often when you receive your most significant breakthroughs, and you will find it buried in the very things you said you couldn't do. The deeper the pain associated with any task you fear, the more profound the change you will experience once it's completed. When you reach this level, your confidence will rise and alert you to a brand-new reality, one you have formed from disbeliefs about yourself, here is where the natural escalation of a human being begins.

'Place yourself in a position of connection and reach for the things that bring you joy, do not be frightened to want that level of enjoyment in your life, for everyone is deserving of it.'

Cultivate the core strength required, and you will thrive in countless situations. Using the information from chapter four to understand the science of the mind, you will find what you need to succeed, ***believe it is in there, for it is!*** Make it your priority to create that attitude, from a safe place filled with trust and integrity, surround yourself with those who also believe in the power of the human bond, and you will live in an environment of support, love, and connectivity. Here you will feel valued and appreciated as the person you were born to be, just as you are, with no expectation to be anything else. The positive outcome of choosing better affects internal chemical reactions, ones that keep body systems in balance and bring synchronisation back to the whole.

'My studies have identified when you are in satisfying relationships; you are better-off, more content, less angry or fragile and your immune systems are a lot stronger, the

evidence makes sense when you have a lot less to worry about.'

The more consideration and time you place on your progress, your learnings, and your growth, the more level-headed you become, which generates the dais for countless choices. You can access that toolbox at any time and select suitable outcomes. Smart people are always open about alternatives and other ideas. They do not allow their egos to get in the way, for they realise no matter who you are; everybody has something to offer and experiences to share. Learn to assimilate emotion and thought together as this raises your internal vibration and pulls what you want to you. Do not get side-lined by anything based on thoughts or interjections from others as this will only create the recipe for your demise. Instead of attempting to fit into a mould, just accept everyone is different, including you and external approval of anything outside of you is unnecessary.

'The best way to change your energy and feel what it's like to live in this space is to hang around with those that elicit these fantastic qualities, for you will never feel small or inadequate in their company.'

There is no competition, only cooperation, motivation, and inspiration when you spend enough time in that tank; it really will have the most profound effect on you, and leave you so pumped you will settle for nothing less. Build new connections with those you would like to learn from, join groups, networking events, social clubs, and evening classes to meet new people and further your learnings.

'Keep reading and listening to positive material that re-programmes negative thinking and gives you a whole new perspective on life. I know it's scary to change something so integral to who you think you are. It is only a place of fear, fear of change that keeps you there.'

Something in your personality must disrupt you enough, and it would help if you listened to it. Every relationship should start with trust; when this crucial ingredient is missing from any union, it can cause stress, worry, lies or deceit. No partnership that is harmonious, loyal, and considerate will ever make you experience any of these. So, listen to your intuition and your heart; they know what's best for you and will always persuade you to take that path. The alternative is your life will be a constant fight to feel as if you are enough. Know this, you were born enough, so take charge!

'When you are fortunate to have a great tribe stay there, treasure them, and bask in the glory that you have found souls worthy of your heart. I hope after reading this book, the learnings will inspire you to want to embrace change,

claiming what was your inheritance at the start of this journey.'

Develop a hunger for knowledge and apply what you find to every aspect of your life. It will lead you to discoveries and synchronicities that will alter your experience forever. Perhaps your choice will inevitably lie in how you will choose to use this information, will it upset you enough to want more and never settle ever again. Starting over becomes an acceptance of your past, one you cannot change and a persistent altered belief for a restored vision moving forward. Invest the time and develop the skills necessary to make it so. I wish to re-ignite that spark within, one that wakes you from your slumber and gets you so stirred, others will begin to wonder what has happened to you. Light that fire by using the information inside these pages and join us on this fantastic expedition.

‘For sometimes you are tested, not towards awareness of your weaknesses but in the direction of your strengths, showing you the way to sculpt your right path, and encourage the elevation necessary to show you what is truly possible in this lifetime. Make it your priority, alter your trajectory today and

‘RISE Strong…’

I have given you the roadmap and shortened the curve to get you there faster; life will never reward your vague wishes, take your time, reflect, and recharge. You will win the game and summit many mountains during your lifetime, remember to celebrate every single victory on your way there. You are not ordinary; you never were, you are amazing, now go get that prize...

Namaste...

The Divine in me recognises the Divine in you.
The God in me meets the God in you.
I respect the soul in you that is also in me.
Irrespective of the language you speak, this word has become world-renowned for the message that lies within. It contains an intelligence, one of sharing and a way to find meaning and connection during our time here.

Your life can be a party, a big celebration; it's your biggest audition for a part you can command the leading role. Seize this opportunity and waste not one moment, for when you do, it becomes the best way to put real meaning into the reason you are here.

'This is the Greatest Show you will ever get the chance to perform in, get excited, get inspired, and if you haven't been sufficiently informed already:'

You are magnificent!

Choose Now, Start Today &

RISE Like A Phoenix Forever...

With my love, gratitude, and blessings for a remarkable life.

Geraldine

You can find more resources in the additional books that work collectively with this one. I have written these as reference manuals to offer practical advice to everyday issues you may be challenged by, giving you real-time information on implementing the changes needed for a better outcome.

Books in the 'Choose to Climb' Series:

100 ways to RISE and Live Your Best Life Volume 1

A reference manual for life's challenges with 100 inspirational passages of clarity, strategy, and direction

100 Ways to RISE and Live Your Best Life Volume 2

A reference manual for a life without limits with another 100 passages to take you beyond your limitations and discover your authentic self.

Book of Inspirational Quotes

Original, never published, inspirational quotes to cultivate positive energy and change the stories you tell yourself about yourself and your life.

'Join the Climb...'

You can also access continuous support through Summit Club. You will find a neighbourhood that nurtures these teachings throughout our global community, hosted by myself and my husband.

Our goal at Summit Club is to bring people together to enrich the lives of each other. We are committed to helping you achieve the goals and lifestyle you want while, having incredible balance and joy in your life.

A global community of likeminded people who help each other grow.

www.choosetoclimb.com

A selection of some additional material that has massively enhanced my journey to an awakened consciousness:

Louise Hay - You Can Heal Your Life
John Assaraf - Having It All
Dr Wayne Dyer – Change Your Thoughts Change Your Life.
Dr Wayne Dyer – Wishes Fulfilled
Dr Spenser Johnson - Who Moved My Cheese
Dr Shefali – The Conscious Parent
Anita Moorjani – Dying to Be Me
Anthony Robbins – Get the Edge
Stephen Covey - The 7 Habits of Highly Effective People
Brendon Burchard – High-Performance Habits
Tom Bilyeu – Impact Theory
Lisa Nichols – Motivating the Masses
Jay Shetty – Follow the Reader
Dr Joe Dispenza - Breaking the Habit of Being You
Dr Joe Dispenza – The Placebo Effect
Dr Joe Dispenza – Becoming Supernatural
Daniella La Porte – White Hot Truth

Be Bold and Rise Strong…

Geraldine

Will You Pay It Forward

If you enjoyed reading RISE Like a Phoenix, would you mind writing a review on Amazon? Even a short one will help, and it would mean so much to me.

If you know anyone who has struggled with self-worth issues or a lack of confidence, please recommend this book to them. Regardless of whether you gift them a copy or tell them where you bought it doesn't matter. All I want is to help those who feel stuck or lost and give them the gift of personal power through these learnings.

If you would like to order copies of this book for any groups, organisations or companies, please contact me directly via email at youcan@choosetoclimb.com to arrange a special discount for bulk purchases.

Finally, if you would like to receive free bonuses and updates on future projects or become a member of our global online support community and gain access to exclusive personal development programs and webinars, you can sign up to our mail list or become a member at www.choosetoclimb.com.

I look forward to hearing from you.

With my Gratitude

Geraldine

RISE, Accept and Soar

Awaken your consciousness to better choices
and a life without limits.

www.choosetoclimb.com

Printed in Great Britain
by Amazon

41720589R00096